Metropolitan Diary

Metropolitan Diary

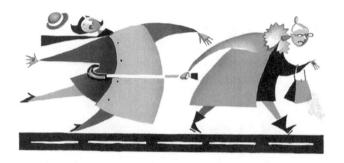

THE BEST SELECTIONS FROM *THE NEW YORK TIMES* COLUMN

Ron Alexander

with illustrations by Susan Romano

WILLIAM MORROW AND COMPANY, INC. / NEW YORK

Library of Congress Cataloging-in-Publication Data

Alexander, Ron.
   Metropolitan diary : the best selections of The New York Times column / by Ron Alexander. — 1st ed.
      p.   cm.
   ISBN 0-688-14889-1 (acid-free paper)
   1. New York (N.Y.)—Social life and customs—Anecdotes. 2. New York (N.Y.)—Social life and customs—Humor. 3. American wit and humor—New York (State)—New York. I. Title.
F128.55.A44   1997
974.7'1—dc21
                            97-7061
                              CIP

Printed in the United States of America

First Edition

1 2 3 4 5 6 7 8 9 10

BOOK DESIGN BY JOANNE METSCH

*To all of the people out there who keep their eyes open
and their ears tuned to the Human comedy,
Metropolitan Diary thanks you.*

Preface

Were you to mix the world of Jules Feiffer with the cast of characters from *Peanuts*, you'd have only an inkling of the anecdotes, observations, light verse, and reminiscences that await you in *Metropolitan Diary*.

The Diary's first entry appeared in November 1976 in *The New York Times*'s new "Living" section; it went on to become one of the paper's most popular features, reporting questions and conversations heard in movie lines, health clubs, theater lobbies, subways, buses, restaurants (delis in particular), cocktail parties, and escalators (especially those in Bloomingdale's). If such items—often referred to by fans as Metro Moments—represent the Diary at its peak—sly, sassy, feisty, funny, often hilarious—be prepared, too, for the more touching items. Consider, for instance, the boy having a heartbreakingly tough time selling homemade lemonade on a late-summer afternoon.

On the other hand, this is what Diary is not: a random collection of anecdotes winding up with the "Only in New York" cliché and a series of exasperated exclamation points. Nor is it a putdown of city people or an outlet for the praise of overzealous grandparents.

Following in the footsteps of fellow reporters Tom Buckley, Lawrence Van Gelder, Glenn Collins, Georgia Dullea, and everybody's favorite understudy, Enid Nemy, I have been keeper of the columns since June 1984.

I have a vague memory of protesting this assignment when presented with it by Alex Ward. Now, more than fourteen years and some one thousand entries later, I can think of few things I would rather be doing. Speaking of which, I am often asked, "You make up the items in the Diary, right?"

Wrong. There are few things as funny as people when they're being serious. Among Metro Diary's staunchest fans are former New Yorkers who rely on family and friends back home to send them their weekly fix of New York City nostalgia.

The *Times* realized the deep affection between readers and Diary some summers ago when the column was dropped from the Sunday national edition. Letters of protest poured in. When the *Times* did an about-face, countless readers wrote in to say thanks.

"Thank you, thank you," wrote a woman from Denver. This from a fellow from Beverly Hills: "It is a Sunday morning, I am having my coffee and I am giving the first section a quick perusal to help me decide whether or not to move on to the hammock. I scan the page-one article regarding upcoming reductions in the military budget, follow through to its continuation on page 18 for the weather report. And then, behold! Metropolitan Diary!! Welcome back!"

Responded *The New York Times* in a letter to readers: "We underestimated the affection people have for the Diary," an executive wrote in a letter of apology, "I hope you will be pleased to see that we have restored Metropolitan Diary to its rightful place in the national edition of the New York news page."

Even I turn up in two items: The scene is the Russian Tea Room. Two women sitting at a table nearby were laughing enthusiastically, when one said, "Sh-h-h-h, we shouldn't be talking so loud, Metropolitan Diary may be near and overhear us." It was, and it did.

And then there was the evening on the Number 10 downtown bus, scene of so many Diary items. The young woman in front of me was reading that week's column. I have never done this before or since, but I could not resist tapping her on the shoulder; "Pardon me," I said, "but can you tell me which item you enjoyed most?" She shot me a strange look and pointed to one of the items. "I'm the editor of the column and was curious," I explained.

A few days later I received a letter from her: "I think you ought to know," she wrote, "there's some-one going around town claiming to be you."

Only in New York?

Acknowledgments

There aren't enough words to thank Marion Donnelly. Without her sense of humor (joyful) and organization (breathtaking) this book would never have been. Without her I would have drowned in a sea of paper.

Still at the top of my list, thanks to Barbara Williams Shelley for her nimble way with technological matters and her knack of convincing me that, yes, I, too, might someday master the computer, though never with the flair she has.

To Robert P. Smith I present the He-Can-Do-Anything-Award to be shared with Jennifer Dunning, master of the Ask-for-an-Inch-and-She'll-Give-You-a-Yard fame. These two can't stop giving. It's good to know when deadlines loom. My sister, June, gave me the benefit of her editorial savvy and her kid-sisterly wisdom.

Georgia Dullea's shoes are not easy to step into. She gave me something to aspire to (beside size ten). As my immediate predecessor, this remarkable woman was not an easy act to follow.

And what can one say about Gwin Chin, except that I am flattered that this wonderful woman about town joined our band bringing along some super ideas and juicy gossip.

Tony Aylward, an actor friend, deserves applause just for being such a fine audience himself.

It is impossible to think of working on this project without Ed Frantz, who gave this book many of its more inspired moments.

I am indeed indebted to Trish Hall for bringing me together with my agent, the soothing Alice Martell. Nothing can really go wrong when the kind and un-flappable Alexandra Palmer is in your corner. And too, James Athas, who never ceased to amaze me with his inexhaustible kindness.

It doesn't hurt to have a therapist, either. Thank you, Howard. Or an enthusiastic co-worker like Mike Levitas. Which brings me to the encouragement of John Montorio and Joe Lelyveld. Thank you, gentlemen.

Contents

Metropolitan Diary

Rising to the Occasion

The place: The elevator in an Upper East Side apartment building.

The time: An evening at the end of a three-day weekend.

Dramatis personae: Two luggage-toting young women, both obviously returning from the shore or country.

Woman One: "So how're the French lessons coming along?"

Woman Two: "OK, I guess. Last week I learned to say 'Thank you, I'd love to go to East Hampton' and also 'I'm very good at husking corn.' "

Woman One, confidingly: "I really don't think you can count on that getting you beyond July."

· · ·

Dear Diary:

It was the evening that workers began demolishing the building on East Fifty-fourth Street that had partly collapsed earlier in the day. I was taking the elevator in my own building nearby to look at the scene with other curious neighbors when an elderly couple got on. He was clearly disgruntled at the notion of having to leave his evening television programs. She, on the other hand, was all set, camera in hand.

He barked, "There'll be lots of asbestos!"

She replied sternly, "We're not going to breathe, we're going to watch."

Nancy Hafter

. . .

Brief encounter in a West Side elevator between two thirtyish women:

Woman One: "Congratulations!"

Woman Two: "What for?"

Woman One: "I hear you're getting married again."

Woman Two: "Oh, that!"

. . .

Dear Diary:

A recent visit to the doctor proved quite disconcerting. Waiting for an elevator in his office lobby, I became involved in a conversation with an elderly woman, who was also going to a doctor. Expressing concern over a rash on her arm, she offered it for my inspection, saying that she hoped it might be poison ivy.

I had no sooner agreed that it didn't look serious when a man—also elderly—stopped, stared, and said, "That looks like Lyme disease."

The elevator arrived, but the stranger pressed on: "Do you have any dizziness? What about pain under your armpits?"

The elevator stopped; the woman got off first, the man right behind her. As they continued down the hall talking, I could hear only bits of their conversation including his "You could die from that!" I must say I was glad when the elevator doors closed.

Robert Embrey

.　　.　　.

Two-woman conversation, overheard by Hank Blaustein of Brooklyn in an elevator at the New School:

"Where are you going?"

"To the Memory course."

"Isn't it on six?"

"No, on five."

"Oh, am I glad I ran into you!"

Airborne

Conversation, in its entirety, overheard on a Boston–to–La Guardia shuttle, between thirtyish male and female:

He: "I just want to know one thing: Have you or have you not been sleeping with Sam?"

She, peering out of window: "I don't care to discuss it over Hartford."

.   .   .

My work necessitates a great deal of air travel, and I frequently find myself seated toward the back of the plane. Recently, waiting to exit a plane that had just landed at La Guardia, I noticed a girl about four or five, standing in the aisle next to my seat.

I smiled. "Is it fun for you to ride on an airplane?" I asked her. She looked up at me, then looked behind her and in a shrill, anxious voice yelled, "Mommy! A stranger is talking to me." I was embarrassed and in my calm, most reassuring voice I said: "You have nothing to worry about; you're with your mom. Sometimes passengers who don't know one another just talk pleasantly when they're waiting to get off the plane."

In an even louder voice she screamed: "Mommy! She's still doing it!" Welcome back to New York, I wished myself. And while you're at it, have a good day.

Christine Lavin

.   .   .

Occasion: A swank fund-raising dinner.

Place: Outside the Waldorf-Astoria's Grand Ballroom.

Dramatis personae: Woman in elegant evening gown, man in spiffy dinner jacket.

Both are huffing and puffing, barely visible behind clouds of cigarette and cigar smoke.

He: "You know what I did when they prohibited smoking on airplanes?"

She: "No, what did you do?"

He: "I bought my own plane."

Wow (Upside Down)

Dear Diary:

At the checkout counter of my friendly local health food store I encountered yet another of the omnipresent baby vehicles that seem to have invaded the city over the last decade or so. My transaction was underscored by the ongoing banter by a cheery mom about darling baby's cuteness, first sandbox experience, and interest in her toes.

I was reminded of my gentleman friend's grandson, a delightful boy of two. I picked up my parcel to leave, beamed at the girl baby, and said to her, "Do I have a boy for you!" To which her cheery mom cooed, "But she doesn't know her sexual preference yet!"

Karen Gibson

.   .   .

It wasn't more than eighteen seconds after the quake stopped. The shaking had finally ended, the house was pitch black, we could hear the last of the crystal rolling off the shelves. In eighteen years of living in California, experience told us that this was a bad quake.

Unbelievably, the phone at the bedside rang. My mother in New York was on the other end of the line.

"So, I hope you're happy," she said. "Now are you going to come home?"

Alan H. Rosenberg

. . .

Lunchtime conversation between mother and grown son in a midtown restaurant, overheard by Jake Wallace Beasley:

Mother: "I went to my doctor yesterday to find out how I can lose some weight."

Son: "I can tell you how to do that. Eat more fruits and vegetables and exercise."

Mother: "That's exactly what he said. But what kind of life is that?"

. . .

Overheard at brunch in a White Plains café:

Mother: "I just keep telling him he needs to quit smoking! What's the big deal? You just take the pack of cigarettes and throw them in the garbage."

Exasperated son: "Ma, it's just not that easy."

Mother: "Oh, please, sure it is. I did it!"
Son: "Yes, but how many times?"
Indignant mother: "Every time!"

Sylvia Williams

. . .

Scene: Street in Belle Harbor, Queens.
Cast of two: Mother and small boy.
"No," Mother says. "I said, NO!" *Brief silence, then:*
"Exactly what is it you don't understand? Is it the 'N'?
Or is it the 'O'?"

Fay Levine

. . .

In New York, survival training begins young.
Mother to a four-year-old, overheard on East Eighty-
third Street: "While I'm getting your Chicken
McNuggets, if someone tells you to get up, just say:
'I'm sorry. This is my table.' "

Helene S. Bell

. . .

Dear Diary:
My daughter-in-law, Laura, was having a difficult
time locating a particular air conditioner permitted in
her co-op apartment. After a futile search through the
Manhattan Yellow Pages, she asked her mother to

continue the search in the Queens directory. A few minutes later her mother called to say she had located the precise model and gave the delighted daughter the number of the retailer who carried it.

Laura immediately dialed the retailer, told him that her mother had just called, and proceeded to quiz him regarding the particulars of the unit. After listening to all her questions, the salesman finally asked, "What's the matter, don't you believe your mother?"

Rhoda Finer

.   .   .

My mother, who arrived at Ellis Island in 1896 (give or take a year), was very proud of her diploma from Public School 62 and her Palmer Method Certificate. Both hung proudly in our home, as we moved all over Brooklyn from apartment to apartment.

With each move we acquired a new milkman and a new milk box. We never met the milkman face to face: he left the milk bottles in the milk box and each week my mother left the money in the same place.

On those occasions when my mother needed to change her order, she sat down at the kitchen table and in her best Palmer Method script wrote a long letter to the milkman. Never did she write: "Leave one quart." Instead, she wrote: "Dear Mr. Milkman, My husband and I wish you to know that we are going to visit my aunt on Saturday. Therefore, please do not leave the usual order. We appreciate all that you do for us, and we wish you, your wife, and your children the best of health, good days, and prosperity."

Then she signed her letter in her fanciest scroll and proudly left the letter in the wooden box.

"You always write to Mr. Milkman but he never writes to you," my sister and I teased her. Accepting our rebukes, she said: "You wait. Someday he will write to me, too. He has too many people and doesn't have time to write to us all."

He didn't reply, of course. And then one day we found a large envelope in the wooden box. Eagerly, we waited for my mother to open the letter. The enclosure was a disappointment to everyone but my mother. After all, she said, he had written to her.

It was a form letter from the milk company informing us that they had changed to a new formula, with a new label. It was to be called homogenized milk.

"You see," said my mother, "he did take the time to tell me he was making a change."

And we never teased her again.

Gertrude Langsam

Reel Things

Irene Deitsch of Staten Island, on one of those never-ending multicinema lines, cannot avoid overhearing neighboring couples.

He, of Couple One, to Couple Two: "So glad you called. Staying home has been so depressing these days."

He, of Couple Two, to Couple One: "I know what you mean. We've hardly moved from our TV set."

She, of Couple One: "I can't take the war: Scuds, bombs, violence. Yet I'm strangely obsessed by it."

She, of Couple Two: "It's the pits. I really need a night out for a change. We're caught up in this Middle East thing."

Curiosity got the better of me. Which of the seven films would they choose? Something light, of course. Something cheery. Something fun. *Alice? Kindergarten Cop?* Boy, was I wrong.

When He of Couple One reached the cashier he slid $30 through the window. "Four for *Eve of Destruction*," he said.

. . .

The scene is Cinema I on Third Avenue on a snowy afternoon. The flick is *Nixon*.

"If this ain't good," John Timko hears a fellow inform his buddies, "I'm out of here and into Bloomie's."

. . .

Dear Diary:

A midsummer night at an East Hampton, Long Island, movie theater. The audience is waiting for the film (*Lone Star*) to start, when almost everyone notices Steven Spielberg walking down the aisle bearing a giant popcorn and soda. This being a cool East Coast kind of crowd, not a comment is heard; there is merely a lot of surreptitious pointing.

A few minutes later, however, when the film starts, there is a problem with the projection, followed by several distortion-filled minutes. Suddenly from the rear, someone yells out, "Hey, Steve, can't you do something?"

Corinne Lande

. . .

Dear Diary:

My wife and I took in a movie at a theater in the East Village. Before heading for the appropriate screening room, we took an escalator to the lower lobby, where there were two public telephones. While my wife was speaking to our baby-sitter on one phone, the other one rang. I answered.

"Hey, man, is Carlos there?"

At that moment, I spotted an usher looking at me. "Hold on," I said into the phone. I asked the usher if he was Carlos.

"No," he said, "but tell them to hang on." He dashed up the stairs.

I told the party on the other end to hang on. I let the phone drop. Moments later, a man with a theater-manager demeanor rushed over to the telephone. Without a word to me, he picked up the receiver. "Carlos is working," he said. "Don't call him here." He slammed down the receiver.

Just then Carlos appeared at the top of the stairs. He looked angry. He also looked much bigger than the manager, who, nevertheless, rushed up the stairs to confront Carlos. Hovering over the manager, he stared him square in the face and said, "Don't you ever do that again or I'll punch you right in the face."

The manager, no patsy, yelled right back. Carlos slapped the manager in the face and the manager rolled down the stairs in a fall that seemed to take at least ten minutes. When he reached the last step, he jumped up and said, "You're fired!" Carlos stormed off. The manager stormed off.

The phone rang again. I answered. "Hey, you, don't ever hang up on me again."

"I didn't hang up on you, but I gotta tell you: Carlos doesn't work here anymore. He just punched some guy who looks like the manager and he got fired."

"Oh, man. You mean Carlos decked Woody?"

"Yeah, I guess."

"OK, thanks," he said, and hung up.

It was time for the movie.

Paul La Rosa

.   .   .

Dear Diary:

The other day we went to see *Apollo 13*. After we settled in our seats, a young couple—apparently on their first or second date—sat in the row behind us. The man asked the woman if she was hungry.

"Get some popcorn," she replied.

"What size?"

"It's a three-hour movie; get me a three-hour popcorn."

When the movie was over, after approximately two hours and ten minutes, I wondered if she still had fifty minutes of popcorn left.

Jack Hartog

Clip Joint

Dear Diary:

I recently took my three-year-old to a Montclair, New Jersey, beauty salon for her first trim. The sign out front read KIDS CUTS $8.

My little girl was tentative about the whole affair, and when I placed her in the booster seat she rocked several times in protest. Still, considering the degree of restraint demanded by the task—remaining calm while a stranger comes at you with a pair of shears, snips dangerously close to your eyelids and behind your back for fifteen minutes, and you barely out of diapers—she behaved beautifully. The hairdresser, who no doubt spends more time moussing matrons than trimming toddlers, apparently felt otherwise. When I went up to pay the tab, the register rang up eleven dollars.

"Your sign says eight dollars for children," I pointed out.

"Yes," said the shopkeeper. "But squirming is extra."

Patricia E. Berry

. . .

Autumn afternoon at a Long Island mall. My daughter Janet was pushing her two sons in a double stroller. The three-year-old had just had his first haircut; the one-and-a-half-year-old was still in curls. A fiftyish woman interrupted her shopping to admire the children.

"What a fine young man and what a sweet little girl!" she cooed.

"They're both boys," their mother corrected.

The woman paused thoughtfully. "Are you sure?"

Sheila B. Blume

. . .

Dear Diary:

While I was having a monthly trim at my favorite barbershop on West Forty-fourth Street the other day, an old college friend, George Goodman, came in and took the chair next to mine. He is better known to the public as Adam Smith, the host of a weekly business program on PBS.

I congratulate him on his recent show about the Internet. His barber interrupts.

"I saw that show, too."

Adam Smith: "Oh? What did you think?"

Barber (with tonsorial gestures): "A little too long in the back."

Nicholas Benton

.   .   .

Dear Diary:

Approaching the tollbooth on the Tappan Zee Bridge, I found myself behind a woman in earnest conversation with the tolltaker. She reached out her car window and handed him her wallet. He removed two bills, then returned the wallet. Next, she handed him her change purse, from which he extracted two coins. He then returned the purse.

The driver was alone in the car. Presumably she had the use of her hands and wasn't blind. I was puzzled.

"I saw it but I didn't believe it," I said to the tolltaker.

He said, "She just had her nails done."

Martin Newman

.   .   .

Dear Diary:

The place is Sal's Barber Shop, First Avenue in the Twenties. A customer comes in and sits down, waiting his turn in silence. Eventually, he looks up and speaks to no one in particular. "We finally heard from the boy in camp," he says. "He wrote to the dog."

James Pearson

.　　.　　.

Dear Diary:

Our friend Natalie is witness to a continuing conversation in a Roslyn, Long Island, beauty salon between the woman in the next chair and the manicurist. With each visit, they discuss the woman's deteriorating relationship with her husband.

Finally, the woman says she is considering a divorce. "What do you think?" she asks.

The manicurist is taken aback. "That's a very serious matter," she says. "I think you should consult another manicurist."

Stan Isaacs

.　　.　　.

Conversation overheard at my Brooklyn Heights barbershop between customer (sitting) and barber (standing):

Customer: "What do you do in the Poconos?"

Barber: "I go there every year."

Customer: "Yes, but what do you do in the Poconos?"

Barber, astonished: "I sit down!"

David Hawkins

.   .   .

A delightful woman of a certain age was sitting beside me as our nails dried at a midtown salon. She struck up a conversation, which led to the following dialogue:

Woman: "What do you do professionally, dear?"

Me: "I'm a ghostwriter."

Woman: "What a coincidence. I work with ghosts, too. What do you write to them?"

Me, surprised: "What exactly is it that you do?"

Woman: "I'm a psychic. I do the Catskills."

Merri Ukraincik

Floor, Please?

Dear Diary:

The elevator in my office building was too crowded for me to reach the button. "Would somebody please press my floor number?" I asked. "It's the same as my age."

One passenger replied, "You better get a job in the Empire State Building."

Joy Rothenberg

.　　.　　.

While waiting for the elevator in a government building the other day, our friend overheard the following: "OK, is this going to be a really big scandal or just a little one?"

Alas, the doors closed before our friend could hear the answer.

.   .   .

Exchange overheard by Norman Franklin of Teaneck, New Jersey, in the up elevator of an office building on Hudson Street.

"Good morning, Marilyn."

"Oh, hi, Ted. Long time no see. Say, that's some tan you have."

"It's jaundice, Marilyn, jaundice."

"Well, whatever."

.   .   .

Conversation between two young women overheard by Patricia Ann Brady in a Saks Fifth Avenue elevator:

Woman One: "I saw your old boyfriend yesterday."

Woman Two: "Paul? Was he alone?"

Woman One: "No. He was with a woman I've never seen before."

Woman Two: "What does she look like?"

Woman One: "She has dark hair and a nose just like you used to have."

.   .   .

Dear Diary:

A crowded elevator in Macy's Herald Square. The packed car stops on the third floor; the doors open. Two friends quickly survey the situation, and one squeezes herself in with us. The second friend stares into the elevator and loudly orders, "Everyone suck it in because I'm getting on!" As I snicker to myself, I hear her proudly inform her friend, "My therapist told me to express how I feel, and I wanted to get on this elevator!"

Christine Harnisch

.　　.　　.

The place: A Bergdorf Goodman elevator. I enter on the fourth floor. A couple, late twenties, are the only other passengers until the third floor, when two middle-aged women, in loud conversation and carrying mink coats, come aboard. I don't intentionally listen to them, but it is just about impossible to do otherwise.

Woman One: "I would never share a bathroom with a man. My mother and father never shared a bathroom. How can anyone share a bathroom? A bathroom is very private. I don't understand young people even considering sharing a bathroom."

Woman Two: "What about Charles? What bathroom does he use?"

Woman One: "Charles never uses my bathroom. I would never share my bathroom with anyone. Charles goes home!"

The elevator reaches the main floor and the two women make a dash for the Chanel boutique. The young man turns to his wife. "I wonder if she minded sharing the elevator with me," he says.

Elinor Franco

· · ·

Dear Diary:

On my way out to lunch, I entered the elevator with two twenty-something women from another office in the Graybar Building, apparently the Siskel and Ebert of fine lunch-counter dining in the area. As we made our way down from the twenty-first floor, I learned of at least three new places to eat on Lexington Avenue.

But as the elevator doors opened, I learned the most important lesson of all.

"Whatever you do," one of them cautioned, "don't get the shrimp platter at Woolworth's."

Jay Sullivan

Tails of the City

On a recent Sunday, one of the more glorious New York afternoons, Nancy Melius was strolling along Central Park West when she saw a man walking his dog. The dog, proudly wagging his tail, carried a long French baguette in its mouth. The dog proceeded to drop the baguette on the sidewalk.

The owner responded by turning to his pet and throwing his hands up in dismay.

"Now how am I supposed to eat it?" he asked.

. . .

Dear Diary:

I was at a red light at Seventh Avenue and Eleventh Street. A man with a very big dog came alongside. I paid no attention until the dog began to growl and bark softly. It was facing me, right paw extended. The man said: "This is Jack. He is introducing himself." The light changed, and off they went.

Thelma Mielke

.   .   .

Scene: Man walking and talking to misbehaving dog, Third Avenue, Bay Ridge, Brooklyn. Olive Reich sees man shaking his finger at dog, while threatening: "If you don't behave I'm going to call 1-800-BAD-DOGS."

.   .   .

The place: Riverside Park, home to vast numbers of dogs and their doting owners. A woman walking near me was pushing a young child in her stroller. Each time the child saw a dog, she went into a frenzy of "woof woofs." Then one I would describe as a "designer" dog—wrinkled and hairless—walked by. The little girl shouted in a delighted voice, "Moo!"

The assemblage, with the exception of the dog's owner, broke into howls of laughter.

Virginia A. Smith

.   .   .

The place: Greenwich Village.
Time: A recent afternoon.
Dramatis personae: Two trendily dressed women, one with her son, who looks to be about five; the other

with a daughter of the same age. Dick Rodstein is witness to the following:

The boy's mother bends down and addresses her son tenderly. "How is your paw?" she asks.

"It feels much better," he answers.

The little girl frowns. "Why are you calling it a paw?" she wants to know. "It's his hand."

"I'm calling it a paw because he's pretending to be a dog," the boy's mother explains.

"Oh," says the little girl gravely. Then she looks into the little boy's eyes and bellows, "Woof, woof, woof, *woof!*"

She looks up at the boy's mother. "I told him I hope he feels better," she says.

*   *   *

Scene: Seventy-second Street and Second Avenue.

Cast: Distinguished-looking gent and two white standard poodles, all three elegantly groomed, walking toward me and my two fuzzy toy poodles.

Spotting the larger members of their breed, the smaller ones begin straining at their leashes, yapping wildly. The bigger versions do not even deign to glance in their direction, choosing to go quietly and purposefully on their way. As I pass them, their owner speaks. "That's right," he instructs. "Ignore them and just keep walking."

Linda Kramer

. . .

Scene: Rockefeller Center.

Dramatis personae: A smartly dressed woman, her dressed-up poodle, and a gentleman who stops to admire the dog. The overdressed pet sports a sweater, a beret, and, on one front paw, a wristwatch.

"Pardon me," the gentleman says, "but is your dog always so dressed up?"

The woman smiles sweetly. "Oh, no," she replies. "Only when we go to see Santa Claus."

. . .

Place: Corner of Bank and Greenwich streets, Manhattan.

Dramatis personae: Man walking a large black Rottweiler; woman walking small black poodle; Elisa DeCarlo, just listening.

Woman, with nod toward big black Rottweiler: "Does he get enough exercise?"

Man: "I walk him twice a day; we have a yard and stairs. He gets plenty of exercise."

Woman: "But does he get enough exercise emotionally?"

. . .

The place is Greenwich Avenue in Greenwich Village, where our friend the dog lover is walking his shaggy mixed-breed. All at once they come upon an adorable-looking dog—floppy, happy, huggable—a type unfamiliar to our friend.

"Excuse me," our friend says to the woman walking the adorable dog, "but just what kind is that?"

"A poodle," she says.

Our friend is surprised. "I've never seen such a soft-looking, shaggy poodle before."

"He hasn't been groomed to look like a transvestite, that's why," the woman says.

"Well, he certainly looks fine," our friend says, turning to go. "By the way, what's his name?"

"Fifi," the woman says.

Family Snapshots

Dear Diary:

Something I think about every Christmas: Brooklyn in the early 1940s. Every Tuesday night was dish night at the movie house around the corner, and by going week after week it was possible to collect a complete set of dinnerware.

Dishes weren't the only premiums offered. My mother collected white porcelain statuettes of presidents and their wives. These figurines, which were about four or five inches high, have become an essential part of my Christmas memories. Under our tree was a representation of the Nativity scene, with the three kings solemnly watching. And just beyond them, also watching, were George and Martha, Abe and Mary, Franklin and Eleanor.

Steve Abbruscato

.   .   .

Dear Diary:

I have kept all the report cards from my two children's school years. I am looking at my son's card from some twenty-five years ago, when he attended kindergarten in Woodbridge, Connecticut. It contains gently worded evaluations of his progress in acquiring the skills deemed necessary to move into first grade (and the world beyond).

"I claim only my share of attention" was one of these skills. "I keep materials out of my mouth" was another.

This is my favorite: "I know how to blow my nose."

Suzanna Lengyel

.   .   .

SANDBOX

Summer was a sandbox
Where we sipped childhood
Through paper straws
While a starfish strainer
Sifted sand
As if it were sugar
And a clown shovel
Fingerprinted pies
With his little white hands.

Clare Muller

. . .

CRAYOLA

My favorite in the box of sixty-four
Was Prussian Blue, rich with its hint
Of green, blue enough to suggest
An exotic nineteenth-century
Militaristic world.
I'd have colored everything Prussian Blue—
Except tree trunks, hands and faces—
But it had to be carefully rationed
Lest, its paper cover stripped away,
It would wear down to nothing.
Without it: prosaic Umber and Sienna,
Yellow-Green, the all-but-useless White.
Adult life, I assumed, is when you own
All the Prussian Blue you'll ever need
To color anything you want.

Lewis Gardner

. . .

The scene: A Madison Avenue bus.

The time: Late afternoon. The stars of this scenario
are two sweet-looking women with silver hair and, it
seemed to a passenger behind them, golden memories.
Clearly in a nostalgic mood, the pair began swapping
reminiscences about sundaes at Schrafft's and somehow segued to the radio programs of yesteryear.

"When I was a little girl," one woman said, "we always listened to *Don McNeill's Breakfast Club*."

"You listened to the *Breakfast Club*, too?" Her companion was overjoyed. "I loved that program! Do you remember that every morning they played a march and Don told everyone listening to march around the breakfast table? What fun that was!"

A sudden silence. Then the first woman said softly, "I never could march around our dining table."

"Oh, my dear," the second woman exclaimed. "But why not?"

"It was up against the wall," her friend said.

E. P. Frantz

.   .   .

A diary entry about a woman who saved her son's first report card reminds Elizabeth Boltson Gordon of Pittsburgh of her own cards, stashed away, dating from the first grade at Public School 175 in Rego Park, Queens, in 1952. She recalls the following.

"The school had opened the year before and was bursting with postwar kids. There were thirteen first-grade classes. Pupils were required to have handkerchiefs on their person at all times. Having no pockets, the girls usually wore theirs pinned to the bodices of their dresses. I still recall receiving my final report card that June. Although I was judged 'outstanding' in 'keeping clothing clean,' 'responding to signals promptly,' and 'doing purposeful work,' I was not happy. I had received a lowly 'satisfactory' in 'using a handkerchief.' "

Ah, the days of yore.

.　　.　　.

A friend writes:

I would like to tell you about Anna.

In her native Warsaw, Anna was a chemist. A few years ago she came to New York to earn more money. She found work as a housekeeper, cleaning apartments with energy and humor.

She worked for a friend of mine and she had Thursdays free, and I hired her the moment I met her. She immediately put my life in order, or as orderly as it will ever be.

We decided that each week we would teach each other one or two words in our native languages. The first week I asked her how to say "hello" and "goodbye." She asked me: "What is miniseries?"

Anna instinctively knows what she should move (loose change scattered on the dresser) and what she should avoid rearranging (videotapes).

She whisks rugs out from beneath my feet, whips curtains from the windows and carries them off to the laundry. She knows where the best bargains on cleaning supplies and clothing are to be bought, sews buttons on my shirts, brews incredible tea, brings life to my window box, walks my dog and shows me photographs of Barry, her German shepherd in Poland.

Anna, who is in her forties, loves New York and is taking an adult education course at Stuyvesant High School, English as a Second Language. Which brings us to another of Anna's loves, the music of Billy Joel.

The way Anna tells it, the first time she heard him sing—the song was "Honesty"—was in all likelihood comparable to the way Ninotchka felt when she sipped Champagne for the very first time.

Each week one of the English as a Second Language students is asked to tell the others about the country where he or she was born. When it was Anna's turn, she asked if she might forgo Poland and talk about Billy Joel instead. Her teacher agreed, although apparently some of her classmates were dismayed.

Nevertheless, she recited some of her favorite Billy Joel lyrics, played a tape or two, and finished to a rousing round of applause and a high grade. Anna's face lights up when she tells the story.

Sometimes Anna talks about returning to Poland for a visit. She misses her husband and friends, she says, and she misses Barry. I understand, of course, but I will miss her, and don't like to hear her talk about it.

"Tell me about Billy Joel again," I say.

.   .   .

THE EGG CREAM

There were ten stools
Covered in red vinyl
That always felt loose
As you twirled around
Waiting for the owner
To begin the process
That was as near to heaven
As you could get
From the contents of a ten-ounce glass;
A practiced sleight of hand; some syrup;
A dash of milk; a spritz of seltzer;
And once upon a time
Some part of an egg.

Ellen Fuchs

When I'm Calling You

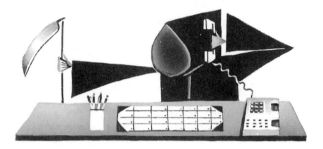

Dear Diary:

My phone call to a cemetery in Saddle Brook, New Jersey, was answered with: "You have reached Riverside Cemetery. If you know your party's extension . . ." Talk about the Internet.

Carol Alexander

·   ·   ·

Dear Diary:

In an effort to inquire about services available for senior citizens in New York City, I began my research with one phone number and was supplied with additional references at each call. One of the agencies I was referred to was named Self Help. After waiting for someone to answer on the other end, I broke out with a smile when the receptionist greeted me: "Self Help. How may I help you?"

Ira Rudowsky

.   .   .

Dear Diary:

Arriving late on a recent dash to La Guardia Airport from midtown Manhattan, I raced down to the last gate on the B Concourse, hurling myself into the jet-way only to come to a screeching halt behind the other hurry-up-and-wait passengers.

As we stood on the long line to the airplane's entrance, a phone on the wall began to ring. It was apparent that none of us had ever seen—or heard—a ringing phone on a jetway, because we all just stood there, eyes glued to the phone, as it rang, rang, rang.

Finally, a chic Kitty Carlisle Hart type glanced at the ringing phone, shrugged her shoulders, and said, "I guess no one's going to answer it." To which she added, "Oh, well, it's probably telemarketing anyway."

Julie Begel

.   .   .

INCOMING CALLS

Phone calls used to count
you knew the people on the other end

their faces
whether they were balding
had a cheerful countenance
smoked a cigar
tapped their fingers

Now, they ring Ring RING
invade our home
and we answer with anticipation
advertising messages
trying to sell me something

My best friend Howard Leibowitz, with the acne,
never tried to sell me anything
in eighth grade.

My high school sweetheart Sarah
with the sweet smile and the dimples
never launched a fund-raising campaign at me,

And now, the worst part of these invasions
isn't that the calls take up my time.
No . . . it's that I don't even know
What these people look like.

Alan Magill

.   .   .

Dear Diary:

We are deluged these days with telemarketing phone solicitations from brokers, storm-door salesmen, and the like. During the day my wife gets the brunt of the attack. The other day she reported one that even I found particularly clever. It went something like this:

Phone: "Ring."

Mary: "Hello?"

Voice: "Is Mr. John Blumenthal there?"

Mary: "No, who's this?"

Voice: (Unintelligible.)

Mary: "Excuse me, I didn't hear you."

Voice: "Miracle Ear Laboratories."

John Blumenthal

. . .

Dear Diary:

In haste, I incorrectly dialed the phone number of a female friend whose son's name is Christian. I heard a strange and unexpected male voice and was not quite certain I had the right number. The halting conversation went something like this:

Other party: "Hello."

Me: "Christian?"

Other party: "Excuse me?"

Me: "Christian?"

Other party: "No, Jewish! What is this anyway, the Inquisition?"

Before he slammed down the receiver, I heard him yell, "Rose, you're not going to believe this last call."

Joseph X. Safina

.　　.　　.

At the recent U.S. Open, during one of Andre Agassi's matches, a man seated in front of us pulled out his cellular phone to call a friend, who was at home watching the match on TV, and said to his friend: "You're watching the Open? We're here! OK, you gotta listen for me."

So when the point had finished, the crowd was silent, and Andre was getting ready to serve, the guy put the phone on his lap and yelled at the top of his lungs, "ANDRE!" He then picked up the phone and said to his friend at home, "Did you hear me?"

Obviously his friend had not. So, again, to the dismay of his wife and those seated around him, he waited until Andre was almost ready to serve and screamed even louder, "ANDRE!" And all the while his poor wife was trying to grab the phone, telling him to stop, covering her face in embarrassment. I'll give the marriage two more years, tops.

Debbie Standish

Screenplays

Dear Diary:

In the closing shots of the film *Emma*, Mr. Knightly and Emma are shown slowly being drawn together by an inevitable, mutual love. The suspense and hushed silence of our audience were shattered by a single remark: "So kiss him already!"

David Abel

.　　.　　.

Overheard in the lobby of a movie theater showing *Pocahontas:*

Grandmother to five-year-old grandson: "I'm so disappointed. I thought John Smith marries Pocahontas."

Little boy, earnestly: "Oh, no, they can't get married. They're different. He's bullets—she's arrows."

Anita Garlick

.   .   .

The current controversy over condoms for high school students took me back to the dark ages of sex education. It was the mid-fifties and in my sixth-grade class in Burbank, California (I now live in Ossining, New York), all the girls, with parents' approval, were to be shown a Walt Disney film on menstruation. (I am not making this up.) The school informed parents, but not students, about the nature of the film, which was animated and, if memory serves, was entitled *You're a Young Lady Now*.

Before the film was shown, there was much secrecy and whispered speculation among the girls. I didn't have a clue, and I begged my best friend, Janet, to enlighten me.

"My mother told me but she said not to talk about it," Janet said primly. "Some of the parents might not want their kids to know."

"Please!" I begged. "I won't tell anyone."

Janet put her mouth close to my ear. "It's about"— she paused for dramatic effect—"administration."

.   .   .

Part of an earnest conversation overheard on Greenwich Avenue in the Village, one middle-aged fellow to another: "You mean to tell me that even after you chose to see Joan Crawford in *A Woman's*

Face rather than John Wayne in *The Fighting Seabees,*
you still didn't realize you were gay?"

.   .   .

Letter from a movie-fan friend:

It was half a century or so ago when I first costarred
with Myrna Loy. It's something I'll never forget: we
were a sophisticated screwball duo solving murders
while sipping martinis. Nor will I ever forget seeing
my name on the same marquee with Betty Grable,
Bette Davis, Kate Hepburn, Doris Day, Hedy Lamarr,
Barbara Stanwyck, Lana Turner, Ingrid Bergman,
Judy Garland, and Ida Lupino.

The key words in this scenario are "movie marquee." For of course I never really made movies
with these ladies (or anyone else, alas), but during
summer vacations from junior high, I worked as an
usher in a theater on the South Shore of Long Island. The programs, revivals as well as new films,
changed twice a week—Wednesdays and Sundays—
and every Tuesday night for an extra two dollars I
would climb a giant ladder, take down the old letters, and put up the new.

Vertigo was all too familiar to me, but I discovered
that by promising myself a treat the climb became
bearable. That treat was putting my name on the marquee alongside the name of the films' leading ladies.

So it was that I starred, for a brief hour or so, in

such classics as *The Thin Man*, *Moon over Miami*, *The Letter*, *Bringing Up Baby*, *Cry Wolf*, *Gaslight*, and *Babes on Broadway*, to name but a few of my biggest triumphs.

Every Saturday night, a fellow usher named Sonny made the week's other marquee change; he started putting his name up there, too. Poor Sonny never got to costar with the really glamorous actresses—his biggest hit was opposite Jennifer Jones in *Song of Bernadette*, which was very boring—and I don't think he was ever in anything in Technicolor.

I bumped into Sonny on Fifth Avenue not long ago, and of course we talked about movies. He said he was on his way home to watch a Gene Tierney picture on one of the movie channels. "You know," he said with a nostalgic smile, "I think I was in that one." We talked about today's actresses, and we couldn't come up with any with whom we would care to costar. Sonny also told me our theater is gone with the wind. "See you on the marquee," he said before heading home. That marquee will always be there, even if it is only in memory. And there's a happy ending: I was in movies when movies were MOVIES.

Turnstiles

Dear Diary:

Subways, crowded as they are, provide fertile ground for the study of human behavior.

For instance, the other afternoon, I was waiting for the southbound R train at Lexington Avenue (Fifty-ninth Street). Just as the train pulled in, the Queens-bound train arrived at the opposite side of the platform. As the trains arrived, I spotted a man, twenty-five-ish and neatly dressed, looking at the two trains. Then he rhythmically pointed his index finger at one train, then the other, and so on, as his lips silently mouthed, "Eeny, meeny, miny, mo."

Stephen M. Banker

·   ·   ·

Dear Diary:

The other day, having taken my seat on the downtown local out of Seventy-second Street, I was surprised to look up and see a familiar face looking at me in the window. After a while, I realized it was my own face, reflected. I proceeded to have a pleasant conversation with myself, by the end of which I found myself folding a paper hat out of the arts page. The strange things one sees on the New York subway.

Roger Rees

.　　.　　.

Dear Diary:

It's the usual morning-rush-hour PATH train from Hoboken to Manhattan. The train makes its usual lurches and jerks as it twists through the tunnel under the Hudson. I have found a comfortable corner spot leaning against a wall. Suddenly, when the train rounds a particularly sharp curve, an eight-foot pole in the middle of the car extending from floor to ceiling comes loose at both ends.

The two women who have been holding on to it look at each other in disbelief; for a few seconds they continue to grasp the pole as though it were still attached to the rest of the car. Everyone stares; no one moves.

Finally, one woman moves toward me and hands me the pole, which must weigh at least ten pounds and is swaying precariously. "I don't know what else to do with it," she says.

I maneuver the pole toward the wall I've been leaning against, slant it slightly, and jam the top into the crevice between ceiling and wall. Then I turn to face it, daring it to move. It doesn't. As we pull into Fourteenth Street, I am reluctant to get off the train, so sure am I that the minute I take my eyes off it, the pole will fall.

Laurie Greenwald Saloman

. . .

Dear Diary:

Riding the Lexington Avenue local one midday, I noticed a woman with a guide dog across the aisle. When the train stopped at Fifty-ninth Street, the dog started to get out. His mistress pulled him back and said curtly, "This isn't our stop."

When the train started again, she was apparently worried that she had been too abrupt and had offended her friend. Oblivious to the other passengers, she said: "I'm sorry I spoke so abruptly. I know that you are not a stupid dog, but that was not our stop. Perhaps you lost count."

The German shepherd looked up at her with close attention during this speech, at the end of which he licked her hand. They got off at Fifty-first Street.

Gene C. Gill

.   .   .

Dear Diary:

Two men—one playing an accordion, the other a violin—were treating the rush-hour audience at the IRT West Ninety-sixth Street station to a performance of classical music. The appreciative crowd tossed coins and bills into the violin case before dashing onto the uptown local when it arrived.

Among the enthusiasts were a young couple with multiple rings in their ears, who couldn't get over the music. I overheard part of their exchange between the screeches of incoming and departing trains.

"That was great!" he said. "In France or Russia they would be considered heroes!" He continued: "I could have sat there with a quart of beer and a pack of cigarettes and listened to them all night."

Wow, I thought. So much for dire predictions about the drop-off in classical music appreciation among young people. Eagerly, I awaited his next comment.

"It sounded just like the music from the Bugs Bunny cartoons I saw when I was a kid."

I decided that perhaps I should not be jumping to optimistic conclusions based on what I overhear on the uptown IRT local at rush hour.

Vivian Awner

.   .   .

The scene: An N train into Manhattan.

The subject: Panhandlers and the lines to get passengers to open hearts and wallets.

Straphanger One: "Remember the guy who wore the same suit when he was begging? We couldn't tell whether it was gray, brown, or dirty white."

Straphanger Two: "Yeah. He said he was dying of some incurable disease."

Straphanger One: "Guess what? I saw him on another train last week. Same rap. So I say to him, 'Hey, you were supposed to be dead a couple of months ago.'"

Straphanger Two: "What happened?"

Straphanger One: "The guy didn't even miss a beat. He kept moving through the car and called back: 'Well, you know. These things take time.'"

Francine Lange

Taxi!

Dear Diary:

I am generally shy about asking cabdrivers to slow down, but when this one went through his third red light and careered around the corner of Broadway and Forty-second Street, I could keep silent no longer.

"Excuse me," I ventured, "would you mind slowing down a little?"

The driver looked back at me. "Whatsa matter?"

"I've been in two cab accidents already," I said.

"That's nothin," he said proudly. "I been in over a hundred!"

Patrick Cook

.　　.　　.

Dear Diary:

Forget about exact change or E-Z Pass. The barter system is alive and well.

The aroma of leftover steak was strong from my friend's doggie bag. Our cabdriver, thin and hungry-looking, pointed to the restaurant we had just come out of and asked whether the steaks lived up to the restaurant's reputation. We assured him the steaks were great.

"Would you like my leftover filet mignon?" my friend asked. "I bet you haven't had lunch yet."

"Oh, I couldn't take your steak," he said. "Unless . . ." His voice trailed off.

"Unless what?" she asked.

"How do you feel about the barter system?" our cabby said. "I'll trade you the ride to Penn Station for your steak."

The bargain made, we proceeded to Penn Station, with our driver happily eating butter-soft filet mignon and french-fried onion rings with his fingers all the way there.

Joan Vitale

•   •   •

Richard Kwartler is a passenger in a Port Washington, L.I., radio taxi when he hears the driver of another cab talking to the dispatcher.

"That kid I just dropped off didn't have any

money," the cabdriver says. "He wants another cab to pick him and a friend up in half an hour to go downtown. He'll pay for both rides then."

"Let me ask you one simple question," the dispatcher replies. "If he doesn't have any money now, what makes you think he'll have any money later?"

"I took his skateboard as collateral," the driver says.

Cast of Characters

Dear Diary:

Seeking ticket information for the show playing at the Houseman Theater, I phoned the box office at 967-7079. In my haste I mistakenly dialed 767-7079.

Pleasant voice: "Good morning."

Me: "Good morning. Is this *Too Jewish*?"

Pleasant voice: "No, it's the New York Athletic Club."

Rabbi Robert A. Alper

●　　●　　●

Scene: The lobby of the Lunt-Fontanne theater, just before a performance of *A Midsummer Night's Dream.*

A patron, deciding whether to wait in line for an infrared hearing device, turns to her companion, and

Lara Holzman hears her ask, "Is there supposed to be a lot of talking in this show?"

.   .   .

A small printed sign was observed outside the auditorium at the CSC Repertory Theater on East Thirteenth Street, where Brecht's *The Resistible Rise of Arturo Ui* is currently being presented:

WARNING

THIS PLAY IS HEAVY.
IT IS ALSO VERY LONG.
IT WILL LEAVE YOU FEELING SAD AND EMPTY.

I wonder what they post when they're doing *The Lower Depths*?

Jeffrey Kindley

.   .   .

Overheard by Marion H. Maidens while leaving the Plymouth Theater following a performance of the Stephen Sondheim musical *Passion*:
Woman to man: "So what did you think?"
Man to woman: "I liked it!"
Woman to man: "You're a liar!"

.   .   .

Dear Diary:

After telling everyone from Santas at Macy's to strangers on the subway that what he wanted most was a violin, my almost-four-year-old son got his wish on Christmas morning. Not a toy, mind you, but a pint-size real-deal violin, on which he has promised to take lessons (although he insists he already knows how to play) and practice, practice, practice. I beamed at his first attempts to make music and imagined him as part of the community of young Perlmans posed on the cover of arts and leisure sections.

I realized, however, that my son was a New Yorker of a different stripe when he handed me a stack of plastic coins from his new cash register and, as he scratched the bow across the strings, instructed me to toss money into his open violin case. Oh, well, perhaps there will be a spot for him on the sidewalk in front of Carnegie Hall.

Tim Lyons

.　　.　　.

Dear Diary:

I recently performed my stand-up comedy act at a center for the elderly in Chelsea. I'm in my twenties and it was no small task to gear my routine to a group with an average age of, say, eighty-five. They seemed to like me; only a few fell asleep. After my act, a woman—probably in her nineties—approached me.

"You, come here," she demanded, much as my grandmother does when she wants attention.

Who was I to argue? A fan's a fan.

"You're the comic, right?"

I nodded proudly.

"Well, I want you to know that I saw Milton Berle when he was your age."

"Yeah . . . wow!" I gasped in mock sincerity.

"Yes," she snapped. "And he was no good either. So stick with it."

There are no easy gigs in New York.

Bill Gordon

Chutzpah

Dear Diary:

While shopping in Loehmann's in the Bronx, with its large, open fitting rooms where women with keen peripheral vision can eye each other's fashion finds and figures, I heard raised voices coming from a dressing-room attendant and a persistent shopper. The customer left in a huff.

"Can you believe her chutzpah?" the indignant attendant asked. "What, no one sews anymore? A needle, a thread—for that she wants another fifty percent off?"

Apparently, the customer had demanded compensation because an already deeply discounted blouse had several loose buttons. After we all acknowledged the brazenness of the stranger and returned to our potential purchases, one of the more vocal sympathizers sidled up to the blouse in question and queried, "How about twenty off?"

.　　.　　.

I can't decide whether to file this under U, as in Urban Resourcefulness, or N, as in New Dimensions in Chutzpah, or both.

I am riding home from work the other night on a Broadway bus, along with two dozen or so other listless passengers wilted from unseasonable heat and humidity. At Seventy-ninth Street, a twenty-something bundle of energy in halter and shorts hops on board, flashes a dollar bill, and (unusually urgently, in retrospect) asks if anyone has change. A Good Samaritan dutifully fishes out four quarters and makes the exchange. The rest of us, half watching out of the corners of our eyes, wait for the clink of coins and the whir of the fare machine to follow as she pays for the ride.

No such thing. Instead, she pulls the stop cord, turns to the driver, smiles sweetly, and announces that she's not going anywhere, she just needed change for the parking meter. She exits the front door at Eighty-second Street. Everyone, including the driver, is too flabbergasted to say a word.

Arthur J. Weiss

.　　.　　.

Dear Diary:

Passing B. Altman's on Fifth Avenue the other day, I was reminded of my last lunch in the store's restaurant, Charleston Gardens. It was in the 1940s, I guess. The restaurant was crowded as usual, and the smiling hostess led an elegant, silver-haired woman toward me.

"Would you mind sharing your table?" the hostess said.

Before I could reply, the woman looked down at me.

"Have you been vaccinated?" she asked.

Smallpox. Altman's. Dowagers. All gone.

C. Libby

. . .

Anyone who has ever taken piano lessons or has ever heard anyone practicing on a piano is surely familiar with the short work for piano by Beethoven called "Für Elise." This is how it goes: da da da da da, da da da da, da da da da, and so on.

Likewise, anyone who has heard a truck backing up has become familiar with the sound it makes. It goes like this: beep beep beep beep beep beep, endlessly. Or at least until the vehicle goes forward or is parked.

On East Seventy-ninth Street the other evening, nineteenth-century music joined twentieth-century technology for an impromptu concert that residents between Second and Third avenues will not soon forget.

Behind the backing vehicle there was a car, foreign and compact. The parking space, as parking spaces in Manhattan go, was ample. Still, the driver was having extraordinary difficulty maneuvering the small car into the ample space. She would go forward, then she would go in reverse, and each time she backed the car up, the neighborhood heard the notes of "Für Elise." Worse, each time it played, the piece started from the beginning. People began peering out windows to watch and wait and listen and shout things like "Shut up with that song already" or "Encore, encore!"

A good while later, success. The car was parked and the strains of "Für Elise" ceased. There was a smattering of applause from some street wiseacres and passersby. Then there was silence and all went back to what they had been doing before the musical interlude.

.　　.　　.

Dear Diary:

In the small town of Port Crane, New York, where my grandchildren live, neighbors toot their horns as they drive by and family members look up from gardens, swings, lawn chairs, or snow shovels to wave hello or to call out a greeting.

Here, in New York City, I walked with Daniel in his stroller and was not surprised by angry drivers blasting horns impatiently. Daniel, almost two, smiled, looked up, waved, and said, "Hi." Bless his country heart.

Mary Anne Christofferson

.　　.　　.

An elderly-sounding woman with a strong Brooklyn accent called my office at Columbia University's department of astronomy to ask about a bright glowing object she had seen "hovering" outside her window the night before. I knew that the planet Venus happened to be bright and well placed in the west for viewing in the early-evening sky, but I asked more questions to verify my suspicions.

After sifting through answers like "It's a little bit higher than the roof of Marty's deli," I concluded that the brightness, compass direction, elevation above the horizon, and time of observation were indeed consistent with her having seen Venus.

Realizing that she had probably lived in Brooklyn most of her life, I asked her why she had called now and not any of the hundreds of other times that Venus was bright over the western horizon. She replied, "I've never noticed it before."

You must understand that to an astronomer this is an astonishing statement. I was compelled to explore her response further.

I asked how long she had lived in her apartment.

"Thirty years," she said. I asked whether she had ever looked out her window before. "I used to keep my curtains closed, but now I keep them open." Naturally, I then asked her why she now kept her curtains open.

"There used to be a tall apartment building outside my window but they tore it down," she said. "Now I can see the sky and it's beautiful."

All in a day's work.

Neil D. Tyson

.   .   .

Cynthia S. Pader of the Bronx is at a bank desk filling out forms. Beside her, a man is busy writing checks and licking a batch of envelopes. As she gathers her finished work, the fellow with the pile of papers glances in Ms. Pader's direction and points to his envelopes and checkbook.

"After I die," he says, "I want to come back as my son."

.   .   .

Dear Diary:

I could see the disappointment on the face of the woman beside me. We were both reading the message on the automatic teller machine: "Temporarily out of service. Please use our other machine at Twenty-first Street." I was about to do just that when I heard a sound of movement within the machine and supposed the reason for the message was that the machine was being serviced from inside the building (which was then closed).

I knocked on the panel and shouted, "How much longer before this works?" The look on the woman's face made me feel like the fellow on *Candid Camera* when he was caught talking to a mailbox.

After my second knock and a repeat of the question, there was a muffled reply from the machine: "It will be working in five minutes."

I couldn't wait, but as I left I looked at the woman's face. "I always suspected," she seemed to say, "there was some little fellow in there counting money."

Harvey M. Rosenwasser

.   .   .

Fragment of a street conversation, department of do-I-really-want-to-know-the-part-I-missed?

The scene: Astor Place.

Dramatis personae: Two women and Steve Rathe, who overhears one of the women, wearing a red jumper with a studded black leather belt, saying, "I told you I was a lesbian."

"Yes," replies her companion, "but everyone says that."

.   .   .

A friend writes:

I'm not particularly religious, but each year on the anniversary of their deaths I light a memorial candle—a yahrzeit—in memory of my parents. The candle, which is in a glass container, remains lighted for at least twenty-four hours.

I usually buy the candles in my local downtown A&P. I know where I will find them, sharing a low shelf alongside borscht and kosher soap.

Recently I found myself in a downtown Food Emporium and checked its shelves in search of the candles. After wandering the aisles in vain, I asked a clerk where I might find the candle in a glass. "I've looked on every shelf," I explained.

"Oh, we don't put them on the shelves," she said. "We display them in our boutique area."

Sure enough, there they were on the floor, displayed with flair, spilling out of chic wooden baskets. Mom and Dad would have gotten a kick out of the sight.

Winging It

Dear Diary:

From my hotel on Central Park South, I often take a morning ramble in the park. Rounding what I call Plaza Pond, near the corner of Fifty-ninth and Fifth, I was startled to see an egret standing on the bank. Tall, elegant, even superior in its manner, this was clearly a Manhattan egret, an egret with attitude.

Astonishingly, this wild bird allowed me to approach within fifteen feet. But being a Manhattan egret, it avoided eye contact and, when I penetrated its critical-distance minimum, flew off.

The next morning, the egret was back, and so was I. And the next. But on Friday morning it was gone. Being a Manhattan egret, it probably flew out to the Hamptons for the weekend.

Terence Smith

. . .

Dear Diary:

Walking to work on a Monday morning, I was preparing myself for a long day in the world of finance.

On Fifty-eighth and Madison I slowed and looked to the sky for some reassurance that I'd be able to survive the long week ahead. I spied a flock of geese flying in V-formation above.

I smiled, and so did the woman standing beside me. "How beautiful!" she exclaimed.

We both stepped to the curb, straining to see the last of the geese.

She informed me that they have to fly very high to make such a formation, and that it's very difficult.

"That made my day," she told me.

"Mine, too," I assured her. The majesty of the geese and the shared moment with a stranger on a busy street in the early morning.

Rachel Markus

. . .

Late afternoon, the Upper West Side:

On Seventy-fourth Street, waiting for the light to change, James F. Horn studies the parade of his fellow West Siders. One woman in particular fascinates him: perched atop her reddish hair is a medium-sized bird. As the woman approaches, the bird takes off to the sky above. Mr. Horn notices the string attached to one of its legs. Suddenly the bird lands on his head. The bird lady grabs the startled Mr. Horn.

"My bird is on your head!" she announced. "I'm so sorry."

Then Mr. Horn stoops down, the woman removes the bird, and she puts it back on her head and goes on her way.

Going Places

The place: A street telephone at Fifth Avenue and Forty-third Street. A college-age woman is speaking. Just as she is about to hang up, another woman, same age bracket, passes by. The two women spot each other and scream with delight.

First young woman: "I can't believe it. I just left you a message on your machine."

Second young woman: "Really! That's absolutely awesome!"

They scream again. Meanwhile, two elderly women observe the scene. As they walk on, one of them is heard to speak wistfully: "I once saw a woman I know in Italy."

.　　.　　.

The time: Approaching midnight, middle of the week.

The scene: Outside Zarela's, a Mexican restaurant in the East Fifties.

Dramatis personae: Two spiffily dressed couples, exiting with good-natured laughter. Time for goodbyes. The women swap last-minute confidences; the men share bear hugs and quick kisses on the cheek.

Nearby two hard-hatted Con Ed workers view the scene. "Gay?" one is heard to ask the other.

"Naah," his buddy assures him. "That's what guys do today."

.   .   .

Dear Diary:

Who says New Yorkers don't care?

It was a sudden, violent accident at Madison and Forty-third. The out-of-control cab skidded across the sidewalk and smacked into the wall of Landmark Stationers and Office Supply. A fleet of police, fire, and assorted ambulance vehicles arrived almost instantly. Two injured pedestrians and the bus driver were quickly attended to. The fruit vendor's cart—a fixture on that corner—was badly damaged, the produce scattered.

By afternoon, all evidence of the accident was gone except for a large patch on the outside wall and, prominently displayed in the shop window, a large hand-lettered sign:

ABRAHAM THE FRUIT MAN WAS
NOT INJURED IN TODAY'S ACCIDENT.

Myron Wald

.　　.　　.

Outside Alpha II, a bar on West Forty-third Street popular among transvestites. Tall, buxom brunette in cutoff jeans and midriff T-shirt, to a sinewy type with shoulder-length braid, tight-fitting fuchsia-colored skirt, and bare midriff: "I told him he was never the man I was."

.　　.　　.

Overheard by John David Earnest on East Seventh Street, one man to another:

"Did you ever stop to consider how different Emma Bovary's life might have been if she'd lived next door to Lucy and Ethel?"

.　　.　　.

Place: Broadway and Seventy-sixth Street.
Players: Debbi Lawrence and Patrick Shea, walking home after dinner.

About to pass a particularly sorry-looking panhandler sprawled on the sidewalk, Debbi stops, reaches into her purse.

Panhandler, studying Debbi, then Patrick, then Debbi again, addresses Debbi: "He was with the other lady yesterday."

Debbi, putting her money back, to panhandler: "Don't quit your day job."

. . .

The scene: Second Avenue in the Seventies.

Players: Affable-looking man, late thirties to early forties; chic, sixty-something woman, soignée, positively Parisian.

The two walk from opposite directions. When their paths cross, the man calls out merrily, "Do you think you could love me forever?"

Her reply (accompanied by a Gallic toss of the shoulder and an I've-been-there roll of the eyes): "Ah, but who loves forever?"

She shrugs again and walks off into the night.

. . .

Dear Diary:

The scene is Fifty-first Street and First Avenue. As the traffic light turns red, a car pulls up on the east side of the street, leaving not enough room for the cars behind to pass.

The driver, a tall, slender young man, gets out of the car and hurries off.

Expecting a burst of horn blowing, shouting, and maybe worse, I look around to see where the driver has gone. It is to the nearest trash basket, in which he carefully deposits an apple core.

Then he hurries back to his car and, as the light changes to green, drives off.

Nobody has been delayed and nobody has said a word. Such a gentle city, New York.

Edwin Newman

What'll It Be?

The scene is a restaurant in Fort Lee, New Jersey. Tobey Karp stops by on her way home from Maine. The soup du jour is clam chowder.

"New England or Manhattan?" Mrs. Karp inquires.

The gum-chewing waitress replies, "Oh, they make it right there in the kitchen."

. . .

Dear Diary:

The scene is the crowded counter of a Starbucks coffee bar on the Upper West Side. I am standing near the counter when I see the coffee server scanning the expectant customers. Thinking he has spotted the right match for a coffee, he innocently asks a man of average height, "Are you the tall drip?"

Startled, the man indignantly replies that, no, he is not a tall drip, but that that is indeed his coffee.

Oh, for the days when we were all simple coffee-regulars.

Jennifer Dann

.   .   .

Recent conversation between Hopeful Diner and Someone at Abe's Steak House on the Upper East Side.

"Hello? I'd like to make a reservation for dinner tonight, please."

"That's fine, but first, how many?"

"Two."

"What time?"

"Seven-thirty."

"For seven-thirty it could be two but not three."

"I said two."

"Everybody says two then two grows into three and three I ain't got."

"I promise, two."

"You're sure?"

"Cross my heart."

"OK."

"Don't you want my name?"

"Nah. I only got one two for seven-thirty."

Click.

.   .   .

Dear Diary:

I recently had lunch with a client at an of-the-moment downtown restaurant. When my guest ordered, the waitress exclaimed, "Excellent choice."

I ordered a different item, which she wrote down without saying anything.

"Don't I get a superlative with my order?" I asked.

She paused a moment, gave me a puzzled look, and said, "Oh, yours comes with mashed potatoes."

Perry Papp

.　.　.

A man we know writes:

We were sitting at a table for two when my wife said: "Guess what? Your therapist is standing near the bar waiting to be seated."

I looked around and sure enough it was he. I turned to my wife and moaned. I looked at the table next to us and groaned. It was free.

I hailed the waitress and said, "See that gentleman at the bar? Please don't sit him next to us. He's my therapist."

"Sure," she said somewhat matter-of-factly, but with a wry smile. "I'll take care of it."

Sure enough (whew!) he was led across the room to another table. We ate, talked, and forgot all about him, when suddenly my wife looked over my shoulder again, this time her face slightly dislocated.

"What?" I asked.

"Guess who just sat down with your therapist? My therapist!"

. . . .

Norman Bressman of Midlothian, Virginia, was at a First Avenue steak restaurant recently when the waiter asked, "What do you want to drink?" Mr. Bressman requested the wine list. The waiter responded: "Mister, I am the wine list. We have a red, a white, and a rosé. Which one do you want?"

Whadjya Say?

To be filed under D, as in And the Dog Ate My Homework. The scene is a No. 2 IRT train. En route to the Brooklyn Museum, Deborah Bornemann and Elaine Koss notice the long delays and stop-and-go motions of their train. Finally, an explanation over the public address system:

"We're sorry for the delay, ladies and gentlemen," a male voice says. "The signals weren't working and our phone was out of order, so I had to go out and use a public telephone and my own Nynex charge card to ascertain that there was a structural defect on the track between Atlantic and Bergen Street. Both the local and express trains have to run on the local track. We apologize for the delay." With that, the train moves on.

.　　.　　.

Dear Diary:

It is 10:30 P.M. and the wearied students from City College's School of Education reach the Fourteenth Street station just as an R train is closing its doors. A young man leaps forward and holds the doors open. Thankfully, we all pile on.

"That's it!" a voice booms over the loudspeaker. "We will stay in this station until everyone learns how to get on and off a train."

Meekly, we sit silently for ten minutes. Then the voice returns: "OK, now we can leave."

The doors close and the train slides out of the station.

Dorothy Mortman

.　　.　　.

During a recent subway excursion I found that I had completed much of that day's *New York Times* crossword puzzle. For the first time ever, I was only four entries away from finishing the puzzle. This, despite the interruptions we have come to expect: "Get your copy of *Street News*." "Extra tokens, anyone?" "You'd help me if I was your family!"

My frustration at being unable to go further brought a vision to mind. I saw myself standing up in the middle of the subway car and calling out to my fellow passengers:

"Ladies and gentlemen! I have been trying to complete *The New York Times* daily crossword puzzle for fifteen years. In all that time I have not got any closer to completion than halfway. Today I am only four entries away from my goal. Won't you please help me find the answers to the four final clues."

The subway reached my stop and the vision faded. I can only wonder whether if I had pleaded for help, my fellow passengers would have come to my assistance. And this, too: If I had acted out my vision, would I have found myself being revealed in someone else's story in Metropolitan Diary?

Abraham J. Katz

.   .   .

Dear Diary:

A group of teenage boys—apparently on their way to school—are waiting to be buzzed through a subway gate. They hold their transit passes for the token booth clerk to see, but her view is blocked by moving people. The train pulls into—and out of—the station while the boys are still locked out. As the train zooms off, they start to yell, and she grabs the microphone and bellows: "You have to be aggressive! You have to be aggressive!"

Phyllis Starkman

. . .

Dear Diary:

It was one of the worst hours of the Big Blizzard when the No. 6 local pulled into the Eighty-sixth Street station. The cars might have just been washed, they looked so fresh and clean. The waiting passengers, however, were dripping with snow. There was a brief pause before the doors opened. Someone, not the conductor, shouted in a very commanding voice, "Wipe your feet before entering!" And by God, many of us did.

George Levine

Celebrity Sightings

Dear Diary:

The recent item from the woman who was recognized after appearing on a television program resonates for those of us who daily emanate from the glowing glass. Recognition, however, takes many forms.

Level One: "You look familiar." I tell such recognizers that I sell shoes and that perhaps they were in my store, Charles Jourdan. Two years ago I committed Level One when I met a former colleague in the Musée d'Orsay in Paris. After the hellos, I noticed a young man off to one side. "You look familiar," I said. "Have we met?"

"No, we have not," he replied, with more stridence than I thought the question deserved.

"Earl," my former colleague gently murmured, "this is Pat Sajac." Oops.

Level Two: "Hey, you're on TV. Channel 5?" I hold up two fingers. "Dennis Cunningham?" I shake my head. This confusion with the arts has been going on for a long time. Twenty-five years ago, I was readily mistaken for Leonard Harris, then the arts editor at Channel 2.

The Level Two dialogue continues: "I know, I know. Health and science?" I smile broadly. "Your name, your name?" If I feel frisky, I say Frank Field. "Nah, nah," my recognizers reply. Somehow they know the difference. I confess. "Earl Ubell. Health and science editor for WCBS-TV."

"Right! I like your reports." I beam broadly. Good for the ratings, I say to myself.

Level Three: On the street I am approached by two women. "Look, Margaret," the nice older woman announces. "It's Earl Ubell."

Her companion, the foolish child, replies with a puzzled frown: "Earl who?" Bad for the ratings, I think.

Level 103: About five years ago, a taxi driver recited my whole work history. "You were science editor of the *Herald Tribune*, and you also worked for WNEW radio. You went to Channel 2 when the *Trib* folded. A couple of years as news director at Channel 4 and back now at Channel 2."

I was stunned. "How did you know?"

"I keep up with these things."
Taxi man: Be fruitful and multiply.

Earl Ubell

.   .   .

A reporter friend writes:

Some years ago, when I was covering the society-celebrity beat, I had occasion to meet Mrs. Onassis three times over a period of three years.

All were for the same cause: to raise money to renovate the New York Public Library building in midtown and to bestow "Literary Lion" awards on well-known writers.

The first time, it took a while before I mustered the courage to introduce myself. When I finally did, she smiled softly and took my noncelebrity hand as graciously as she had those of Russell Baker, John Gregory Dunne, and Joan Didion. She spoke of the library's glories and gave me a suitable quotation or two. "If you feel they need polishing, I trust you," she said. I sometimes think she winked, but I guess not.

The following year I requested another comment and suggested that we change the subject from the library to, say, animals. "A number of writers are being honored tonight as 'Literary Lions,'" I said. "If you had your choice"—gulp—"what animal would you like to be?"

Mrs. Onassis looked at me as if I were crazed. "Oh,

dear!" she said with a sigh. "Can't you just repeat what I said last year? No one will remember." (I'm positive that was followed by a confiding wink.)

We dropped the subject of animals and moved on to fashion. "Who designed your dress?" I asked.

She said she didn't like such questions. I told her that I didn't either, but that my editor did. "All right," she said, relenting. "It's a Valentino."

I avoided fashion at our third, and final, library encounter. I pushed my reporter's notebook deep into my pocket and walked over to her.

"I always know that each year I'm going to see you at this event," I told her.

"How nice," she said. Then, with concern, she asked, "But what do you do the rest of the year?"

.   .   .

Dear Diary:

Last Wednesday, while walking downtown, I stood cooling my heels at the crosswalk at Fifty-seventh and Fifth as a six-car motorcade—part of the anniversary celebration for the United Nations—turned south against the light.

As the first limousines passed by, I couldn't help wondering why officials inside the cars were grinning and waving at me. So I peeked behind me, and there at my elbow, tall as the Statue of Liberty, was Donald Trump. He was crammed on the sidewalk along with the rest of us. When the last limo had made the turn,

I looked up and said, "You'd think they'd stop for you."

As he took his first stride to cross, he winked and said simply, "You'd think."

Doug Shenson

.　　.　　.

It is 11:00 P.M. on a Sunday on the Upper West Side. A couple in their forties are walking two Labrador retriever puppies.

She: "Did you see who that man was?"
He: "No. Who was he?"
She: "Mandy Patinkin!"
He: "The governor?"
She: "No, the actor!"
He: "Oh."
She: "So much for being a celebrity."

.　　.　　.

Dear Diary:

Strolling through Central Park on a recent Saturday morning, I stumbled upon a Sierra Club–sponsored bird walk. Since I had a pair of binoculars around my neck, I decided to join the group.

We walked around the lake, then headed for the Ramble. "The finest place in the park for birding," said the guide, who added that the best spot in all of New York City was Kennedy International Airport, whose vast stretches of uninhabited land attract all sorts of birds.

As we proceeded through the wooded area, two young men in the group were discussing their finds. Apparently they had just made a sighting.

"What did you see?" asked a woman with large binoculars.

"We saw Bruce Willis, Demi Moore, and their children," one of the young men said. "Didn't you see them?"

"No," the woman said, "but I just saw a cardinal."

The other young man smiled. "That's just as good," he said.

Andrew B. Potoker

.   .   .

Scene: A theater-district boîte.

Time: Late Saturday night, during the weekend of the United Nations celebration.

Dramatis personae: Three young male theater types, very likely dancers, discussing rumor and fact.

Fellow One: "I heard Yeltsin was at *Sunset* tonight."

Fellow Two: "The foreign minister of Egypt and the king of Latvia were at *Victor/Victoria.*"

Fellow Three, quietly: "I saw my periodontist and his wife in Shubert Alley."

.   .   .

Dear Diary:

As a fan of vintage Hollywood films, I certainly knew of the career of Guy Kibbee, the 1930s character actor. Among his many roles, he was the kindly old lighthouse-keeper in *Captain January* who fought to keep Shirley Temple from being taken away, and he played Babbitt in the movie of the same name.

Still, I was not prepared for the fellow on the No. 1 train the other afternoon. He moved toward me conspiratorially and announced in my ear, "Guy Kibbee lives on a kibbutz in Joplin, Missouri."

In New York, one learns the darndest things.

Bruce Deal

. . .

Middle of a conversation overheard on Madison Avenue between an irritated, well-groomed woman and an equally annoyed well-groomed man.

She: "So self-important! Who does he think he is?"

He: "He's the brother-in-law of the king of Spain, and his wife is the king's sister, that's who!"

She: "Oh."

Diary File

To be filed under A, as in After Newark, What? After changing trains there, Jim Bungerz listens as the conductor announces with assurance: "This is the six-fifty-sev . . ." Pause. "This is the six-forty . . ." Pause. "This is the six-something train to Raritan Valley."

.   .   .

To be filed under A, as in Ain't Love Grand, or perhaps L, as in Love Is Where You Find It. At any rate, the scene is an elevator in the Brill Building, 1619 Broadway. I enter in the middle of a conversation.

Thin guy: "This afternoon, I've got to look for a Valentine gift for my wife."

Heavyset, bearded guy: "My wife only wants a wheelbarrow and some manure for Valentine's Day. She also wants a rototiller, but that has to wait."

Thin guy: "You live on a farm?"
Heavyset, bearded guy: "God, no! Upper West Side."

Wanda Donnelly

.   .   .

To be filed under T, as 'Tis the Season for Traffic Jams:

The other afternoon, a friend of ours, in a rush to get crosstown from the East Side, hopped in a cab. A few snail-paced blocks later he realized the error of his ways.

"I should have walked," he said to the cabdriver.

"Yeah," the driver agreed. "And I should have been a doctor."

.   .   .

To be filed under R, as in Relative Merits:

Fifty-something woman on phone, incredulous: "Four? Four? I'm number four on your speed dial? How can I be four?"

Ellen Steinbaum, nearby, overhearing, thinks: Get a life. Why would you care what number you are on someone's speed dial?

Woman on phone, still incredulous, whining slightly: "But I'm your only child!"

.   .   .

To be filed under W, as in Widening Generation Gap. Doris L. Meyer of Livingston, New Jersey, is telling a young friend about a woman she saw in a restaurant.

Doris Meyer: "She looked just like Eleanor Roosevelt."

Young friend: "How do you mean?"

D. M.: "She had those nibbly little lips and those big teeth."

Y. F.: "Wow, did you actually know her?"

D. M.: "No, I used to see her in the newsreels."

Y. F.: "Was that on cable or regular TV?"

D. M.: "Forget it."

.   .   .

To be filed under E, as in Everyone's an Expert in Old New York.

At the Brontë exhibition recently at the Pierpont Morgan Library, we peered delightedly at minute manuscripts, locks of hair, and drawings.

An elderly woman with a European accent leaned over a case and announced with great authority, "You know, they changed their name from Prontë."

"With a P?" her companion asked uncertainly.

"Yes, absolutely."

For a moment, I considered checking. Who knew?

Kathryn Bonn

.   .   .

To be filed under W, as in Who's on First?

The place is a crowded M10 bus heading down Seventh Avenue. Of the many conversations going on, one between two middle-aged women is heard above the din. Their chatter becomes even more animated as the vehicle approaches the electronic billboard outside Madison Square Garden.

Woman One: "Oh, look! Neil Diamond is coming here in August."

Woman Two: "Oh, I love him. His plays are a riot."

Woman One: "No, no. You're thinking of Neil Simon."

Woman Two: "Oh, yes. The one who used to sing with that other guy—you know, what's-his-name?"

Woman One: "No, no. That's Paul Simon. He sang with Garfunkel."

Woman Two: "Right. *His* name I can remember."

May I Help You?

Dear Diary:

Searching through the maze of Bloomingdale's with a friend who had to find socks to go with the shoes she had just bought, I stopped in front of a young clerk handing out store guides. The following conversation occurred.

Me: "Excuse me, where are socks?"

Guide: "They're at Fiftieth and Fifth."

Me, puzzled: "Socks?"

Guide, insistent: "Yes, Fiftieth and Fifth Avenue."

I asked the next guide where I could find hosiery.

Linda Przybyszewski

.　　.　　.

Dear Diary:

My daughter—a high school senior—was cast as the nurse in *Romeo and Juliet*.

Wanting to mark the occasion, I nipped into the local Toys "R" Us for a doll dressed as a nurse, to which I could attach the note "To my favorite nurse, love, Mom."

I headed toward a floor-to-ceiling display of dolls. Alas, no nurse. Alert to a customer's bewilderment, an employee approached me. I asked if the store carried any nurse dolls.

"It's a present for my daughter," I explained.

He walked me to a "Dr. Barbie" doll.

"I want a nurse, not a doctor," I said. "Aren't there any dolls dressed as nurses?"

"Lady," he said, miffed, "this is 1996. They're all doctors."

"But I want a nurse."

"Lady," he said again, more annoyed than before, "you got to have higher aspirations for your daughter. You shouldn't want her to be a nurse when she can be a doctor."

I thought it best not to explain about Shakespeare or, for that matter, my high regard for the nursing profession.

Duly chastened, I left quietly, smiling.

Jane Paznik-Bondarin

·   ·   ·

Friday is my day to run errands, and this is what happened last Friday.

10:00 A.M.: At Lord & Taylor with a dress I had bought the day before. I hadn't noticed it was missewn. Annoyed, I wait for the seamstress. She appears and says: "No problem. I'll have it fixed in half an hour. No sense in making you take another trip to pick it up." She returns in twenty minutes. The dress is perfect.

11:00 A.M.: Down to Thirty-Second Street to have the zipper on a leather handbag repaired. "Give us an hour and I'll have it done for you," the proprietor says. "Save you a trip back." I return at 11:45. The zipper has been repaired and I am on my way to the Research Library.

4:00 P.M.: I stop for a glass of orange juice at the little bakery café set up on the terrace of the library. The manager hands me a large round loaf of bread. "Would you like this focaccia?" he asks. "I'm closing up now and I'd rather give it to you than let it get stale." The bread is delicious.

4:30 P.M.: At the bus stop, carrying my bread, my handbag, and my perfect dress, a woman hands me her transfer.

"I'm going to walk," she says. "You may as well use it."

Was this day the exception to the rule? Or is New York becoming a kinder place? I look forward to further evidence.

Annette Henkin Landau

. . .

Dear Diary:

During a recent lunch hour, I rushed out to a mega-bookstore to buy a new book on retirement. Not finding the book in the personal-finance section, I asked the fellow at the information desk if the book was in stock. He checked it out on the computer. "It should be on the shelf," he said.

When I insisted it wasn't there, he offered to find it for me. I followed him as he whizzed past personal finance and stopped several aisles away. Sure enough, there was the book. In the death-and-dying section.

I made two quick decisions: not to buy the book and not to retire.

Marianne McNamara

. . .

Dear Diary:

Buying a T-shirt at the Pop Shop in SoHo, I asked the cashier what to me was a common question after purchasing an item.

"Do you wrap?"

The puzzled cashier paused, while I wondered what was so complex about the question. At long last, he replied:

"No, but I like listening to it. Why do you ask?"

Richard Dalton, Jr.

Scenes

Overheard one evening in the vicinity of Lincoln Center, one man to another: "Well, shall we run through Tower Records and pick up Peggy Lee?"

.   .   .

The constant companion of Martha Little's granddaughter is a furry gorilla. It is named Pig-Pig and is almost the same size as the youngster, who has her heart set on acquiring Pig-Pig No. 2. Mrs. Little, who lives in Baltimore, has been searching for such an item with little success.

One recent inspired day, she remembered F.A.O. Schwarz, the long distance no obstacle. She telephoned the store and asked the operator for stuffed animals.

A moment later a deep voice was on the other end of the line. "Bears," he announced.

"Hello," Mrs. Little said. "I'm looking for a gorilla."

"That," the deep voice replied, "would be Jungle Animals," and that's where Mrs. Little was promptly transferred.

.　　.　　.

The time: A Sunday afternoon on Avenue of the Americas in Manhattan.

The place: Bed, Bath and Beyond, the vast store that seems to have everything. Two beyond-middle-age women in the housewares department are uncertain about that.

"You know the thing I'm looking for?" the first woman says to her companion. "I've been looking for it all over and I can't find it anywhere. I don't think they make it anymore."

"What happened to yours?" her friend inquires.

"I gave it to you," the first woman says.

"No, you didn't," the second woman replies.

There is a pause and a shrug of her shoulders before the first woman speaks again.

"Oh, then it must have been Cheryl," she says.

The two head for another department without letting an eavesdropper learn what it was.

Transfer, Please

Late afternoon. I was sitting next to the window on a bus heading downtown for Pennsylvania Station. Traffic was exceptionally heavy.

When the bus stopped for a light at Thirty-eighth Street, I saw a friend at the corner waiting to cross.

I called her name—"Bernice!"—through the bottom of the open window. She looked around, but the sun was shining on my window, and she couldn't see me.

The bus moved ahead slowly, and when it stopped for the next light, my friend was waiting to cross the street.

"Bernice!" I called again, and again she looked around but couldn't see me.

At a third light, Bernice was standing on the corner.

For the third time, I called her name. She looked around so frantically I couldn't resist.

"Bernice," I called. "Repent."

Helene Bell

.   .   .

Dear Diary:

The other morning I boarded the M4 Fifth Avenue bus at Eighty-fourth Street. It was crowded, and a number of passengers had to stand. At Seventy-ninth Street, an elderly man boarded, and a younger woman rose to give him her seat. Two stops later, he gave the seat to another woman. "Are you sure?" she asked.

"We're playing musical chairs," he assured her, a twinkle in his eyes.

"Well, in that case, we'll need some music," she said. With that, she proceeded to sing, sotto voce, the "Habanera" from *Carmen* in its entirety.

When I was reluctantly readying my exit, I'm sure I heard a castanet and a tambourine or two. It was a nice way to start the new year.

Alvin Thaler

.   .   .

The other evening, as the No. 10 bus bumped its way down Seventh Avenue on its way to Battery Park City, it was apparent that something had been added to the journey: a chorus of coughs, sniffles, and assorted other signs and sounds of winter head colds.

"Boy, do I feel lousy," one woman said.

"I can't wait to prop myself against the pillows and sip endless cups of hot tea," another woman replied.

The first woman shook her head in disagreement. "When my throat is dry and scratchy," she said, "what I most want is deliciously cold Jell-O."

"Jell-O?" woman No. 2 said, clutching her throat. "When you have a cold you want chilly Jell-O? How strange!"

"No, no," woman No. 1 insisted. "It's perfect. And two-sixty a pound is, I think, rather reasonable."

"You make a pound of Jell-O? Would that be individual servings?"

"No, I buy a pound of Jell-O in the deli. Someone else makes it."

"You can't make Jell-O?" Woman No. 1 seemed horrified.

"Of course I can make Jell-O, but I choose not to make it."

"It's so easy," woman No. 2 said. "All you need is hot water."

"I know that," woman No. 1 said, standing up to exit at the next stop.

"It's so easy," woman No. 2 shouted after her. "Ask anyone."

The doors closed; the bus began moving. The

woman turned to the couple sitting in back of her. "She can't make Jell-O," she said sadly.

.   .   .

Dear Diary:

When getting off a bus, I thank the driver and wish him a nice day. There is usually a return "Thank you, you, too."

Yesterday, on a not particularly crowded vehicle, I assumed the driver did not hear me and I repeated, "Thank you, have a nice day."

"Lady, I heard you the first time," he said.

Evelyn Winkler

.   .   .

Dear Diary:

I was on a somewhat crowded crosstown M79 bus around 4:00 P.M., and I was standing in front of a well-dressed woman and her equally well-dressed young daughter. As the bus slowed to approach a stop, mother and daughter rose.

"Now, dear," the mother said, "remember what I taught you to say?"

Pleased to be witnessing an example of manners, I smiled, waiting to hear the daughter's reply.

She opened her mouth, and in a sleep-shattering voice yelled, "Getting out!"

Gail Janowitz

Weather or Not

Dear Diary:

I'm one of those New Yorkers who must be near concrete on summer weekends. I love having the city to myself, free to go to theaters, movies, restaurants. The throngs have rushed to the country.

On sunny days I often sunbathe on the sidewalk in front of my apartment building, stretched out and comfy in my chaise, lapping up the warmth of the sun.

I actually convince myself I'm at a posh resort. There is calm in the air, few cars, little noise.

Last weekend as I was sunning, a woman walked down my block, saw me in my reverie, and asked politely, "How's the water?"

Bobbie Kaplan

. . .

Dear Diary:

On one of fall's warmest days, an errand took me past the frozen yogurt shop on Lexington Avenue near Eighty-sixth Street.

I was tempted, but resisted. Didn't need the calories. Probably no good for my retirement-age body.

Came the return trip. Who could resist twice in one day? I savored a vanilla cone as I strolled down the avenue.

Waiting for a light to change, I heard, "Mmm, that looks good." The speaker: a woman sharing the moment.

Resisting a strong urge to offer her some, I confessed: "It is. I decided I deserved it."

She smiled. "If not now, when?" she said.

James W. Johnson

. . .

Dear Diary:

As one who works at home I find myself, on the nicer days of New York's notoriously fickle spring, maximizing the number of errands I have to perform, rather than trying to be efficient and get everything done in one trip—though not without a certain amount of guilt.

During a recent warm spell, a neighbor seemed to have the same idea. I ran into him with embarrassing regularity as I was entering or exiting my building. After what seemed to be our umpteenth encounter, he finally spoke to me.

"We have to stop meeting like this," he said. "I'm gay. You're straight. People are going to talk."

Joan Haladay

.　　.　　.

Dear Diary:

It was a few days after the initial big blizzard and I longed to socialize again. But where do you socialize in icy weather in Canarsie? Eventually I ventured out, but having reached an intersection I could go no farther. Standing there, stranded, I looked around for help.

Finally, I spotted a woman walking carefully. I knew her casually, but for the life of me I couldn't remember her name. I did remember, however, that she loved mah-jongg.

So I began to shout, "Mah-jongg, mah-jongg!" Sure enough, the woman turned around slowly, bewildered, no doubt, to see what the yelling was all about. I beckoned to her for assistance. Saved at last!

I shall never again cross Shore Road without hearing the echo of my own voice shouting "Mah-jongg, mah-jongg!" somewhere in the distance.

Pearl Ganx

●　　　●　　　●

Dear Diary:

It is 6:00 P.M. on Day 2 of the Blizzard of '96. I am walking past the fountain in front of the Plaza Hotel, admiring the effect of fresh snow on the pine trees. The man walking in front of me is smoking a cigar.

An approaching man pauses and tells the smoker, "You know, cigars and snow don't go together."

The cigar smoker turns to him and responds, "Oh, but I think they do."

What follows surprises me. They both smile a moment and go their separate ways. This prompts the question: Were they tourists or was it the snow?

Sandra Yin

●　　　●　　　●

January 1, 1996, 10:00 A.M. The city's streets are quiet yet the sounds of Christmas remain in the air. Walking along East Eighty-eighth Street, I detect a few faint bars of "Silver Bells" and "Deck the Halls." I look around. Not a Christmas tree in sight. Could the melodies be coming from a car alarm? Unlikely. As I saunter home I spot the source of the belated holiday serenade: a synthesizer about the size of a quarter, a miniature orchestra softly but distinctly playing its program.

It had probably been discarded with a tree and a string of colored lights, but was left behind after the garbage collectors had come and gone. And so, though Christmas had been over for a week, the band played on.

Loraine Heller

Just Kidding

Dear Diary:

A bustling Saturday afternoon on Columbus Avenue. I notice a well-dressed family—mother, father, two girls about three and five years old—strolling leisurely. The parents are talking to each other, the girls to each other. A sudden spat between the girls, and the smaller one gives vent to a piercing shriek. Father scoops up the sobbing child and Mother bends to talk to the older one.

"You must learn to share with your sister," Mother says. "Now, tell me, exactly how many Slime Things do you have? If it is two or more, give her one."

.   .   .

Dear Diary:

The other day at my local Nobody Beats the Wiz, the throngs of holiday shoppers fell silent: the wail of a child's tantrum fixed the crowd. Then a gruff voice soared out, "Somebody give that kid a gift, will ya?"

Howard Milkin

.　　.　　.

Dear Diary:

Young students from the School of American Ballet were rehearsing for their professional appearances in *Coppélia* at the New York State Theater. While they were onstage polishing their steps, they left their belongings outside the orchestra level in the hallway.

I walked through this hallway the other day, and there on the floor was a clothing label that read DKNY and right next to it a discarded Tootsie Roll wrapper.

It's nice to know these budding ballerinas aren't growing up too quickly.

Joyce Jaffee

.　　.　　.

Dear Diary:

Kimberly, our four-year-old granddaughter, has a lively imagination and a sense of humor, so her parents were not surprised when after seeing *Beauty and the Beast* she announced, "From now on, I'm Belle." This was fun for a week, but as months passed, her insistence that she was Belle became tiresome. You can imagine her mother's relief when Kimberly announced, "When I say I'm Belle, I'm just pretending." After a pause, she added, "I'm really Pocahontas."

Robert A. Wofsey

.   .   .

Conversation between a mother and a son, who looked to be five or six, on upper Madison Avenue at lunchtime, overheard by Robert E. Moore of Hopewell, New Jersey:

"Mommy, I know what I want to be when I grow up."

"Yes?"

"I want to be a writer and a sidekick."

The mother hesitated a moment or so and said: "A sidekick? What's a sidekick?"

"It's a detective that looks into the future."

"No," the mother said. "You mean a psychic."

"Yes," the boy said. "A sidekick."

.   .   .

A sun-drenched Saturday at Shea Stadium. The Mets are losing 2 to 0 when the home-team bats suddenly come alive. As the fans begin to clamor for runs, Anita Dente and Margaret Doria overhear a voice fraught with the dual frustrations of the Mets fan and the dad:

"Second and third and no outs, and *now* you have to go to the bathroom?"

.   .   .

Dear Diary:

Overheard in an Upper West Side sandbox one recent Saturday afternoon, between a mother and three-and-a-half-year-old son, Elijah, who was busy with shovel, truck, and pail:

Mother: "What are you doing, Eli, building a road?"

Son: "No, I'm repairing a water-main break."

Joan Lebow

.   .   .

Nehama Zibitt was explaining the omnipresence of God to her kindergarten class at the Hebrew school of Congregation Ohav Shalom in Merrick, Long Island.

"Is God in your bedrooms?" she asked.

"Yes."

"Is God in your kitchen?"

"Yes."

"Is God in the den with you when you play Nintendo?"

"Yes," they said, giggling now.

Ms. Zibitt then explained that God was even in places outside the home.

"God is even in Waldbaum's," she said.

"Which aisle?" piped up one little girl.

Wise Guys

Dear Diary:

The scene is the Fairway Market on upper Broadway, where a busy-looking professional mom is picking over mountains of fruits and vegetables. Her daughter, about six or seven, dressed in frills and bows, is dancing in the aisle, humming to herself.

"Do you know what song I'm humming?" the girl asks.

"No, sweetie," Mom replies.

"Try to guess!"

"I don't know, dear."

"Beethoven's Ninth!" is the enthusiastic reply.

Stephen M. Smith

. . .

Dear Diary:

Something tells me I'm raising a true New Yorker. At four and a half, my daughter knows all about gargoyles and skylights, croissants and latte, and how to get dinner using the telephone and a paper menu.

She knows what to do when the car is blocked by another that is double-parked (honk and swear a lot), how to arrange a play date (even though she calls them "play days"), and exactly where to look in the harbor for the grandest of sights: Lady Liberty.

She knows that macaroni and cheese tastes best when eaten out of bowls on the front stoop with friends, that Joe the fruit and vegetable man always has strawberries or grapes for a smiling or crying child, and that you can run like the wind but you must stop well before dinner or your mother will become very grouchy.

But there are many things my daughter has yet to learn. After exuberantly singing along with a new music tape the other day ("I'm walking in the mall, I'm walking in the mall/Now I'm going home . . ."), she looked at me, perplexed.

"Mom," she asked, "what's a mall?"

It makes a mother proud.

Stephanie Steib

.   .   .

Dear Diary:

I was walking with Jeremy, my grandson, when a stranger stopped in front of us and asked, "How old are you, little boy?"

"Three," Jeremy replied.

"And when are you going to be four?"

"When I'm through being three."

Bob Kaye

. . .

Dear Diary:

My just-turned-six granddaughter, an apartment-dwelling Manhattanite, was visiting me in East Hampton, Long Island, for a four-day weekend. At breakfast on the last morning of her visit, she put down her cereal spoon, sighed wistfully, and said, "I miss Mommy and I miss my doorman."

Felice Wiener

. . .

A friend writes:

Before my six-year-old girl was to enter public school, I attempted to enlighten her about the birds and bees. "I want to tell you something," I started. "It's not the stork that brings the babies."

"Ha," she said. "I've known that for a long time."

"Is there anything more that you want to know?"

"Yes," she said. "How do you make paper?"

.   .   .

Dear Diary:

On a recent visit to the Whitney Museum of American Art to view the Biennial Exhibition, my friend Edward Smith and I saw a group of grade-school youngsters touring the galleries with their teacher. The teacher called the class to a halt in front of a large oil painting.

"Does anybody remember which artist painted this?" we heard the teacher ask.

At first there was no response. Then a look of recognition gradually swept across the face of one little boy and he began waving his hand furiously.

"Yes?" the teacher said, pointing to him.

"Willem de Kooning!" he shouted for the entire museum to hear.

"Very good!" the teacher said. "How did you remember? Was it from our trip here last year?"

"No," the boy replied. "He lives next door to us in the Hamptons."

Renee Bacher

High Neighbors

This is what happened the other day.

Richard locked himself out of his West Fourth Street apartment. The super wasn't around. Two hours later, Richard was still waiting in the lobby. Then Mary Anne, an upstairs neighbor, came home. She didn't have the keys to Richard's apartment, but she had keys to Carol's apartment next door to her. And Carol, she knew, had keys to Lydia's apartment on the floor below. And Lydia, Richard knew, had keys to his apartment.

So Mary Anne used her keys to get into Carol's apartment, where she found a set of keys labeled "Lydia." Then Mary Anne and Richard went to Lydia's apartment, where Richard was certain he would find the keys to his apartment. And so he did. A few minutes later he was unlocking his own door.

There's a moral here someplace, maybe about good neighbors, maybe about New York apartment dwellers. On the other hand it could be a question. Like, didn't Lucy and Ethel have it easy?

Jane Heil

.　　.　　.

Martine J. Byer, riding in the elevator in a friend's prewar Upper West Side apartment building, overhears the following from the elevator's other occupants:

Man: "You don't live here, do you?"

Woman: "Not yet, but I'm engaged to the man in 6C. We're getting married in June."

Man: "Congratulations. You're moving into a very good building."

.　　.　　.

Dear Diary:

The other evening I spotted the following note posted on my lobby door:

"To whoever's cat(s) is creating this unholy stench in the building, please do something about it. It is beginning to permeate apartments. Thank you.

"Your Fellow Tenants."

Knowing full well the source of the problem, and resenting the possible aspersions cast on my own two cats, I posted this reply:

"I suspect this may be your first spring on East Third Street. Each year the trees in the back flower; the flowers drop, and the rain and heat combine to create that delightful aroma. It is known as 'The Stinky Green Flower Season.' Be patient. It will pass.

"A fourteen-year Veteran of the Building."

Later, I was pleased to find the following note of support posted:

"*Generic name:* weed tree.

"Brought over from Asia, mid-1800s. A durable, extremely hardy, highly adaptable, and efficiently self-propagating species that thrives on neglect, poor soil, and the verbal abuse of mankind. Drops small greenish blossoms in late spring, which tend to be overly fragrant, especially when soaked with favorable and abundant rainfall."

. . .

A fellow we know, estranged from his wife, returns to have dinner in the Upper East Side marital apartment for the first time in eighteen months of separation. He is greeted warmly by the doorman, who says how happy he is to see him again, adding that his wife is a wonderful woman and that he hopes our friend will soon be coming home. There is the briefest of pauses and the doorman speaks again.

"And we're getting all new windows," he says.

Growing Pains

Dear Diary:

I live in Heritage Village, a serene, relaxed adult community in western Connecticut.

Greeting two of my neighbors—dignified Helen Hokinson types—laboriously maneuvering out of their car, I heard one confide to the other:

"Do you know what I can't do anymore? I can't skip."

Ah, youth.

Annie Rossoff

.　　.　　.

The ticket holders' line at a midtown Manhattan movie. The majority of these filmgoers were the G-rated crowd and parents. Among the exceptions were two women of a certain age who, it was apparent, had just met.

"I have to confess something to you," the first woman said. "I have never felt as foolish as I did when I stepped up to the box office and said, 'One for *Thumbelina*, please.' "

"It could have been worse," her new friend assured her. "I asked for 'one for *Thumbelina* and please don't forget the senior discount.' "

.   .   .

Dear Diary:

A rather healthy but apparently not so virile elderly gentleman strolled into the operating room for correction of his problem. As the anesthesia resident in the operating room that day, I examined his chart as I prepared him for the anesthetic.

According to the preoperative questionnaire he had filled out, he was in terrific medical shape: he had answered no to all of the routine questions. However, under the section asking patients to "list all current conditions," he had simply scribbled, "In love."

Michael Locker

.   .   .

THE LAST ECLIPSE

A week ago Tuesday, the appropriate place to be—judging by the size of the crowd—was the plaza in front of the Hayden Planetarium. There several hundred people gathered eagerly to view the solar eclipse.

Among them: a threesome of Brandeis High School students interviewing several elders, including Gabriel Grayson, a faculty member at the New School who also lectures at the American Museum of Natural History. One student interviewer, age about fourteen, armed with a video camera and microphone, approached Mr. Grayson. "Can I talk with you?" he asked shyly.

"Sure," the bearded, balding, fiftyish professor replied.

"Uh, you're old, like forty, and won't be around for the next eclipse in eighteen years," the interviewer said earnestly. "How does it feel to be here at your last eclipse?"

The professor smiled. "Do you work with Barbara Walters?" he asked.

.　　.　　.

Scene: The Austin Street Senior Center, Forest Hills, Queens.

Dramatis personae: Two silver-haired women, and Rose F. McArdle, who overhears their brief conversation.

Woman One: "Your hair looks lovely today. Is it a wig?"

Woman Two: "Yes."

Woman One: "You'd never know it."

Gotta Have Art

The scene: "The Machine Age in America 1918–1941" exhibition at the Brooklyn Museum. Among the group peering at one of the display cases is a middle-aged woman who lets out a gasp. She nudges her companion and waves at a set of brightly colored plastic-handled flatwear, circa 1930.

"Look, Shirley," she says. "And I've been using mine for everyday."

. . .

Dear Diary:

Before making a reservation for my Fashion Institute of Technology drawing class to see the "Picasso and Portraiture" exhibition, I learned that three of the twenty-five students had never been to the Museum of Modern Art. All of them, however, turned up in the museum's crowded lobby, and I began a hurried overview of Picasso: his work, wives, mistresses, and children.

Suddenly, one of the twenty-year-old students came alive: "You mean that this guy is related to Paloma?"

Katherine Bradford

.　　.　　.

Having just overlooked the sign and arrow pointing to the Toulouse-Lautrec exhibition at the Metropolitan Museum of Art, I hastened to one of the guards and said casually, "Hi . . . Toulouse-Lautrec?"

He smiled. "Hi . . . David Coolihan!"

Anna S. Lee

.　　.　　.

The place is the "Art of the Forties" exhibit at the Museum of Modern Art. A woman among the viewers stares intently for quite a while at a photograph of Martha Graham. After some time she looks around for the friend she came in with; she finds her stationed in front of a large oil painting.

"Oh, for Pete's sake, Sheila!" the first woman calls out in a loud voice. "Come and see this; there's more to life than Edward Hopper, you know."

.　　.　　.

The scene: The Jewish Museum gift shop on a crowded day. I am looking at the shelves of menorahs and sculptures. A girl, about six, looks up at me and asks, "Do you know who made that?" She is pointing to a colorful metal dreidel on the top shelf.

I tell her that I don't know. "My dad did," she replies. An imaginative child, I think, until I see behind her a beaming bearded man nodding that he is both her dad and the artist. I compliment him and move on.

As I am leaving the gift shop I look back. Father and daughter are still there, staring proudly at the dreidel on the top shelf.

Harold Langus

.　　.　　.

In town from Connecticut for the day, Joyce Greif heads for the Metropolitan Museum of Art. In the course of her visit she makes a telephone call. The phone beside her is occupied by a beefy thirtyish fellow outfitted in a parka, blue jeans, boots, baseball cap, the works.

"New York is boring!" he fairly shouts into the phone. Then: "Where am I? Where am I? I'm in the Metropolitan Museum of Art!"

All Around the Town

I am at the "appetizing" counter of the local suburban supermarket, having ordered a half-pound of Nova. While the ponytailed counterperson dons white surgical gloves in order to detach the precisely presliced lox from the hermetically sealed plastic container, I reminisce about the Saturday morning some thirty-two years ago when I was a newly married nineteen-year-old living with my young husband, a law student, in a small apartment on Kings Highway in Brooklyn. I approached the formidable Waldbaum's appetizing counter for the very first time.

As I waited that day long ago, my number was finally called. I looked up to see the chief of the appy department—a grizzled veteran of the whitefish and pickled-herring wars—eyeing me with complete and utter boredom, knowing, I'm positive, that I was a total novice compared with the accomplished mavens who had ordered before me.

"What'll it be, lady?" he asked. I proudly said, "Half a pound of Nova and a quarter-pound of belly." Wordlessly and glovelessly, he began to carve slices of lox with a very long, wickedly sharp knife. He wrapped the delicacies in white butcher paper and wrote the price with a black crayon.

"There's your Novy," he said.

I said, a bit anxiously: "Excuse me, but are you sure that's the Nova? It looks very light. I thought the Nova was darker in color."

He lifted his craggy head, looked me in the eye, and, loud enough for all of Kings Highway to hear, said, "Lady, you matching a dress or buying lox?"

Thoroughly humbled, listening to the chuckles of everyone around me, I mumbled something of an apology for doubting his expertise and fled the counter as soon as the order was completed.

I must admit that from that day forward I've been slightly intimidated when taking my ticket at the appy counter, never knowing whether I'll get an order of embarrassment and humility with my Nova.

Jacqueline Frank

.　　　.　　　.

New Jersey suburb scene: Four sixty-something couples study the menu at a Chinese restaurant. One of the women takes an embroidered eyeglass case from her purse. Her friend notices and comments favorably on the handiwork. "I got it in Wales," the woman replies. "We didn't shop big there."

Laurie Goodman

.   .   .

The place: The Barnes & Noble, West Paterson, New Jersey, cookbook section.

Dramatis personae: Husband and wife (overheard by Mildred Hathaway of Totowa, New Jersey, among other browsers).

Wife to husband: "For my next birthday, I'd like this cookbook."

Hard-of-hearing husband: "What?"

Wife, louder: "I'd like this for my birthday."

Husband: "What?"

Wife, no longer sotto voce, full-voiced: "This book! My birthday!"

Browsers look up and in unison start singing "Happy Birthday to You."

Wife to browsers: "Not yet. It's in October. I'll be sixty-five and eligible for Medicare."

Browsers: "Great!" "Hurray!" "Wonderful!"

.   .   .

Dear Diary:

We ordered a birthday cake from our local bakery in Millburn, New Jersey, to celebrate our father's ninety-seventh birthday. The bakers there do not decorate the cake until you arrive to pick it up and pay for it.

We instructed the baker to write "Happy 97th" on the cake. The store was crowded when the baker, holding up the pink and the blue pastry tubes, asked above the din in the store, "Is this for a boy or a girl?"

Jean L. Banks

.　　.　　.

Scene: A supermarket in West Orange, New Jersey.

Dramatis personae: Attractive woman with neatly coiffured blond hair; she wears a pale blue pantsuit. She walks up and down the aisles very slowly, a result of her surgical collar and three-pronged cane. A box of cereal is tucked under her free arm.

She looks up and recognizes another shopper.

"Helen?" she says.

"Beverly?" the woman says uncertainly. "I haven't seen you in ages. How have you been? You look terrific! Keep in touch!"

Dorothy C. Goldberg

.　　.　　.

The scene: The music department, Barnes & Noble, Ridgewood, New Jersey.

Dramatis personae: Two salesclerks, assisting a young male customer, and Seymour Sally, who witnesses the little session.

Salesclerk One: "He's looking for something performed by Beethoven. Did he perform anything, or did he only write music?"

Salesclerk Two: "If he did perform, we wouldn't carry anything he did: he was deaf."

. . .

Dear Diary:

The scene is a home furnishings shop in Norwalk, Connecticut. The shoppers run the gamut of ages; the clerks are young and eager.

One clerk shouts across the shop, "What time is it?"

Second clerk replies, "Quarter to three."

With that, a half-dozen or so sing out:

> "It's quarter to three,
> No one in the place
> Except you and me . . ."

Smiles break out all over, except on the faces of the two bewildered young clerks.

Happy birthday, Frankie!

Roy Doty

. . .

Overheard at the cat-and-dog-food aisle of a suburban Connecticut supermarket, a mother speaking to her nine-year-old daughter, who was pushing the cart:

"Don't go down that aisle. We don't have any animals in our house—except, of course, your brother."

.　　.　　.

Dear Diary:

In the perfume department at Macy's, Kings Plaza, Brooklyn, a woman in a hooded parka with a capacious tote bag picks up a silver-coated item from a cart stacked high with silver-coated Calvin Klein items.

An anxious young man steps from behind the cart, snatches the item from her, and asks, "May I help you?"

"I'm looking for Calvin Klein's Obsession."

"For men or women?"

"A woman, of course."

"But these are Calvin Klein Unisex!"

"Oh," the woman mutters as she turns to go, "I haven't any unisexers on my list."

Nancy Finley

.　　.　　.

Dear Diary:

I live in Freeport, Long Island, with my wife, who loves to go shopping for bargains in the town's thrift shops. I entertain myself observing the customers, most of whom are genuinely seeking to stretch a limited budget, while others seem to be killing time in Freeport.

One day, as I sat observing the traffic, I spotted someone who so closely resembled the Princess of Wales that my eyes fairly popped. I stared a bit, then, dusting off and polishing my almost-forgotten skills at mild flirtation (I am eighty-two years old), I stepped up and said: "Princess Diana. What are you doing in Freeport, New York?"

The young woman gave me a delicious little giggle, then, with that distinctly Diana clipped British inflection, said:

"I was talking to the Duchess of Sudbury the other day and mentioned I needed a little housedress, but I didn't want to go to London shops. They make such a fuss.

" 'Have you considered Freeport, New York?' Sudsy asked. 'Understand they have the best shops in the world.'

"I hopped aboard a Concorde to Kennedy, jumped in a limo, and here I am."

This last was said with a twinkle.

Just as I was saying, "I hope you find what you want," my wife showed up and asked to whom I had been talking.

"You'd never believe me," I replied.

Herbert Jaffe

Relatively Speaking

An exchange between mother and daughter, heard while waiting for a bus outside the Morris Brothers store, Broadway and Eighty-fourth Street:

Daughter, about ten or eleven: "How come when you take me shopping, we always go to Morris Brothers, but when you go alone, you go to Bloomingdale's?"

Mother: "Because I'm training you for Bloomingdale's."

My bus came, and they disappeared into the store.

Mark Korman

. . .

Dear Diary:
   Son: "Do you want to play Gold Fish?"
   Dad: "It's Go Fish."

Son: "No, it's Gold Fish."

Dad: "Who is four and who is forty?"

Son: "Well, I am four and a half and you are forty-one and it's Gold Fish."

Dad: "Let's play."

Gregg P. Monsees (forty-one)

.　.　.

I was strolling down Madison Avenue early one morning when I overtook a young man pushing a stroller and patiently coaching a boy surely no more than three years old.

"What's on top of South Dakota?" the father asked.

"North Dakota," the child replied.

"And what's on top of China?" the father pressed. Silence.

"Mongolia," the father supplied forcefully. Then, "And what's Down Under?"

"Finland!" the boy said with certainty.

"No," the father answered as they crossed the street. "Australia."

Just fifteen years until the SAT. It's never too early to prepare for a perfect score.

Harrison J. Goldin

.　.　.

Walking along Central Park West, I hear a conversation coming from behind me. A family of four heads for a picnic in the park; the most outspoken member of the quartet is a little girl about eight years old.

"I want to change my name," she announces.

"But why, Amanda?" her brother, about eleven, asks with concern.

"That's why!" she replies. "It's not Amanda, it's Aman-DUH. Everyone says 'Aman-DUH' and it's getting embarrassing. Wouldn't you get tired of hearing 'DUH' all day?"

Joe Baldwin

.　　.　　.

Two women were discussing furniture and furnishings when Robert Seilman overheard them on a Broadway bus.

Woman One: "Did you like your son's new house?"

Woman Two: "Yes. His wife is especially proud of their Early American furniture."

Woman One: "So, do you like it?"

Woman Two, uncertainly: "I don't know. I'm old-fashioned. I like new furniture."

.　　.　　.

The other day, two women walking in front of me discovered they knew each other slightly and began to chat.

Finally, one asked, "How is your husband?"

"Better than the last one!" was the response.

Anne Sager

Getting Off, Please

Dear Diary:

Riding the M2 Limited down Fifth Avenue, I am listening to a lively conversation between two fellow passengers. She was proudly displaying the contents of a brand-new knapsack from the Gap. He was polite, if noncommittal.

"So when are you going to be in kindergarten?" she asked, an older woman of six or seven.

He seemed not to know the answer. Then he piped up, apropos of nothing, "My grandpa died."

She looked at him and, nodding, said: "My grandmother died, too. She's in the Gates of Heaven."

My heart warmed to hear such a sweet way of visualizing her grandmother's passing.

"What's the Gates of Heaven?" he asked.
"A cemetery in New Jersey," she replied.

Valerie Steiker

.　　.　　.

Snippet of determined crosstown bus conversation: "I don't care if she is on Prozac and if she is a recovered alcoholic. She's still a bore."

.　　.　　.

Conversation overheard by Hinda Gonchor going downtown on an M104 bus:
First woman: "Didn't we meet a while back at an Indian meditation meeting?"
Second woman: "Yes."
First woman: "I haven't seen you lately. Do you still go?"
Second woman: "No."
First woman: "How come?"
Second woman: "I don't know. I just stopped."
First woman: "Did you chant at home?"
Second woman: "No. I only chanted at meetings."
First woman: "Then you didn't get any of the benefits. You must chant at home to get all the benefits. It's essential."
Second woman: "Have you gotten many benefits?"
First woman: "Have I? I just got a one-bedroom six-

hundred-dollar-a-month apartment on Eighty-sixth Street near Broadway."

Second woman: "Oh. That's really something."

． ． ．

The scene: A Madison Avenue bus.

Dramatic personae: Two women, obvious bus acquaintances, and Helen M. Donovan, who overhears their conversation.

Woman One: "Isn't this rain awful? It goes on forever."

Woman Two: "It's good for the crops."

Woman One: "Who has crops?"

． ． ．

The scene: Northbound Riverdale bus.

Dramatis personae: A driver, three riders, and Anna S. Singer, who listens to them.

Rider No. 1, to driver: "Can you tell me the stop for Wave Hill?"

Driver: "Nope."

Rider No. 2: "The stop is 245th Street."

Driver: "What's so special about Wave Hill?"

Rider No. 1: "There are beautiful gardens and flowers. The view of the Hudson is superb. Also, Toscanini lived there."

Driver: "Toscanini?"

Rider No. 2: "He was a conductor."

Driver: "Oh. Train or bus?"

.   .   .

On the Manhattan-bound Green Bus Line Q60, a conversation between a woman and her thirty-something daughter suddenly became loud enough for Peter LaMassa to hear.

"But Ma, you don't have to tell your friends that Michael and I are living in sin. Just tell them we're living in Rego Park."

Dining Out

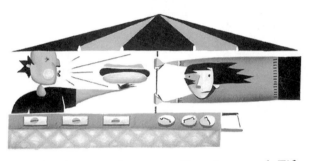

Scene: Hot-dog stand, corner Broadway and Fifty-second Street.

Dramatis personae: Vendor, diner, and Rowana Shepard, who overhears them.

Diner, pointing to hot dogs: "Are they hot?"

Vendor: "Yeah."

Diner: "I want them warm. I don't want them hot."

Vendor: "I'll blow on it for you."

. . .

Overheard by Roberta Cha at the Festival of Food deli on Main Street in Port Washington, Long Island, customer to counterman: "One everything bagel . . . with nothing on it."

. . .

The place: An outdoor table at Sanzin restaurant, Spring Street at Thompson.

Observer: George Zito.

Events: Mother with strong French accent speaks to toddler son who is sitting on building steps.

"Alexander, this is New York. You can't lick the steps."

    •   •   •

Dear Diary:

On the subject of lunch: Running late on my way to a job interview, I decided to brown-bag my meal and spring for a cab.

The midtown noon traffic was terrible, and it became clear that I would need to eat my fat-free yogurt en route. Gradually, I became aware of a pungent odor emanating from the front seat and realized I wasn't the only one who had planned ahead; the driver had unwrapped what smelled like a liverwurst and mustard on rye.

We inched our way down Fifth Avenue, the silence broken only by the rustle of paper napkins, tinfoil, and plastic each time we hit a red light. At last we reached my destination. As I opened the taxi door the driver waved goodbye and spoke for the first time.

"We must do lunch again sometime," he said.

Alicia Farrell

    •   •   •

Dear Diary:

My friend and I decided to carry my newly purchased kitchen table onto the subway to avoid having to pay taxi fare to Brooklyn. Sweaty and exhausted, we sat with the table in front of us.

The woman beside us leaned over. "So, what's for lunch?" she asked.

Amy Gershenson

.   .   .

For a recent birthday dinner at a Spanish restaurant in Greenwich Village, the birthday girl's roommate, Danielle, had baked a birthday cake and brought it to the restaurant. When the time for dessert arrived, she asked the waiter to bring out the cake, to which he responded, apologetically, that the cake had "fallen in the paella."

Amused but annoyed, we decided we were entitled to some compensation for this mishap. However, when Danielle went in search of the waiter, she discovered that her cake was in fact being consumed by a second birthday gathering in that same restaurant!

So, as any New Yorker would, she liberated the remaining corner of the cake for our enjoyment—but not before being told by the other birthday revelers about their surprise at the homemade taste of the restaurant's cake.

Harlan J. Protass

.　　.　　.

Dear Diary:

Departing Parioli Romanissimo, the posh, pricey Italian restaurant in an Upper East Side brownstone, my wife and I were delighted at having to step over a flier at the front door that turned out to be a Chinese takeout menu.

Bill Van Dyke

.　　.　　.

Dear Diary:

I enter a small Italian restaurant at Ninth Avenue and Fifty-Seventh Street on a Monday evening. As I seat myself, a self-confident middle-aged woman at the table opposite mine is about to leave. The background music is Julio Iglesias singing "La Paloma" in Spanish.

The woman turns to me and says, "Funny hearing Russian music in an Italian restaurant."

"That's Spanish," I reply.

"Russian," she insists. "He's singing 'Ochi Tchorniye.'" With that she begins singing her version of "Ochi Tchorniye," imagining that she is replicating the melody on the loudspeaker.

Now I know my Spanish from my Russian, and my "La Paloma" from my "Ochi Tchorniye." But it is the end of a long day, and the lady is self-confident, and does it really matter?

"Well, you never know what you'll hear in New York," I say.

She smiles a victorious smile and walks out of the restaurant. To the strains of "La Paloma."

Robert J. Penella

Shop Talk

The place: D'Agostino's, Lexington and Eighty-third.

The players: Aristocratic mature woman; perky younger woman. Relationship unknown.

The dialogue, as heard by Jim Speer:

A.M.W.: "Oh, look! A very good special on toilet tissue."

P.Y.W.: "What colors does it come in?"

A.M.W., *firmly:* "Toilet tissue, like candles and dinner napkins, should only be white."

P.Y.W., *uncertainly:* "Well, actually, the paper I'm using now is white. But it does have little blue swans on it."

A.M.W.: "Oh, my God!"

.　　.　　.

Dear Diary:

Trying to fit holiday food shopping into my tax season schedule, I rushed into my supermarket in Bayside, Queens, and asked the first clerk I spotted, "Where is your Passover aisle?"

She thought for a moment, then answered, "I'm sorry, but in this store we just mark down."

Janice Temple

.　　.　　.

While Joseph Salderelli was at the grocer's the other afternoon with his wife, he found himself sorting through the corn for perfect ears. Having found them, he saw from the corner of his eyes that a shopping cart had pulled up beside him. He began to put his corn into the cart, assuming that it was his mate's.

"Excuse me!" the cart driver said. Mr. Salderelli looked up and saw an elderly woman about to begin her own search for corn.

"I'm sorry," he said. "I thought you were my wife." The woman cast a sly glance in his direction.

"You wish," she said.

.　　.　　.

Dear Diary:

When my wife calls me with my weekly shopping list, I hastily grab the closest piece of paper, which usually turns out to be my prescription pad. It is this list that I was quickly surveying on the way to the checkout counter at Glick's Kosher Butcher in Forest Hills, Queens. I realized that I had forgotten to get flanken, the meat used for our traditional Sabbath dish. I asked the butcher if there was any available in the case. He glanced curiously at my list and said, "I didn't know you need a prescription for flanken."

Seth G. Friedman, M.D.

. . .

Dear Diary:

An older gentleman watched me judiciously selecting pears at Dean & DeLuca recently. "How do you tell when they'll be ripe?" he asked.

"Well," I replied, "it's hard to say: a day, maybe two."

"But how do you know? I never get pears; I never know when they'll be ripe."

I passed on someone else's wise words about there being only ten perfect moments in the life of a pear and then, rather sternly, I added my own philosophy: "When the pear is ready, you have to be ready."

The gentleman looked longingly at the fruit in my basket, then timidly chose two pears from the pile in front of him. When they were bagged and weighed, he handed me his business card.

"Look," he said, "when yours are ready, will you call me?"

Thomas Lee

.   .   .

Dear Diary:

Walking west on Spring Street toward SoHo, I ducked into a Korean grocery. A white Rolls-Royce pulled up to the curb. As I paid for my purchases the driver of the Rolls (white suit) got out and deliberated over two trays of melon. Loudly, he called out to the passenger in the car, "Honey, which do I like, the green or the orange?"

The window of the Rolls glided halfway down and a woman's face appeared.

"The orange is cantaloupe; the green is honeydew," she said.

The man in the white suit dropped his hands to his sides in a gesture of exasperation and, teeth clenched, said: "I know what they are. I asked you what do I like."

Ted Lee

The Lineup

Dear Diary:

Yesterday, the checkout line in the Riverdale Food Emporium snaked to one end of the store in the deli department. All aisles were clogged with shopping carts. It was a chaotic but friendly atmosphere as people commented about the storm outside.

Suddenly, I became aware of a commotion started by a man forcing his shopping cart through the line. Evidently he had scraped more than a few ankles and received more than a few sharp words. Nevertheless, he continued on.

Then I witnessed how little it takes for someone—probably a perfectly rational person at other times—to go berserk. He raised his two-wheeled shopping cart above his head, upending it. Burritos, Parmesan cheese, canned and paper goods crashed to the floor.

Fortunately, there were no glass products. Without a downward glance at his previous necessities now scattered about, he folded his cart and stalked away.

Those who witnessed the incident were surprisingly understanding of the fellow's behavior, speculating about a wife who might have considered the things strewn about absolutely essential and about what might happen when he arrived home. We wondered aloud if he would be asked to go out into the storm and repeat his ordeal in another neighborhood. It was food for thought on a winter night.

Ida Wyman

. . .

Marla Schaefer is standing in a movie line in the Sheepshead Bay area of Brooklyn when she overhears one elderly woman say to another: "If I'm alive next year, I'm not going back to Dr. Schecter."

. . .

Dear Diary:

On October 31, Halloween night, between buying pumpkins and heading home to carve them, I stopped at the White Plains Department of Motor Vehicles to renew my driver's license.

I was greeted at the door by a woman dressed as a pirate. She handed me a form to fill out and ushered me inside toward Cleopatra. Cleo took my picture, gave me a card, and pointed me in the direction of the DMV line, the bane of every driver's existence. After a forty-five-minute wait, the woman behind me cracked in the face of bureaucratic inefficiency: she left the line to inquire why there were six people behind the counter when only two of them appeared to be doing anything. Thus we learned that Donald Duck was a trainee and as such was not allowed to work on her own, and that the cocktail waitress, the Spiderwoman, and the DMV mascot, complete with paper tiara and license plates dangling from her neck, were supervisors and therefore not allowed to help people. That left all the work up to the Queen of Hearts and Rudolph the Red-Nosed Reindeer.

The woman rejoined the line to resume her wait. I was left wondering if the overweight spaghetti chef and the NFL player were loitering staff members or confused motorists who didn't know which line to join.

Emily Moqtaderi

· · ·

Dear Diary:

The other morning I accompanied my fiancé to the Department of Motor Vehicles while he renewed his New York driver's license. Recalling my own recent experience in renewing early last September, I told him it shouldn't take more than twenty minutes. The process required a photo, vision test, and renewal fee. Two or three clerks were working, the same as in September.

Three hours later and still in line: why the delay? Then it occurred to me. The individuals now renewing before their birthdays were all Geminis: carefree, garrulous, and disorganized. When I renewed, we were all Virgos: our sun sign manifested in a dour procession of purpose, order, and efficiency.

Yikes! The wedding's off!

Juliet Levesque

. . .

In Forest Hills, Devy Goldstein is on a luncheonette line for a morning coffee-to-go. While waiting, she hears this conversation between the counterman and his wife:

Counterman: "You know, I haven't seen Herb in a long time."

Wife: "Herb who?"

Counterman: "You know, Herb!"

Wife: "I don't know who you're talking about."

Counterman: "No milk, two sugars, eight-fifteen."

Wife: "Oh, that Herb. Gee, I hope he's OK."

. . .

Dear Diary:

Some weekends ago, after subway tokens had gone from $1.25 to $1.50, I waited in line at the Union

Square station with just enough money for two round trips and a one-way. When I stepped up to the window and requested five tokens, I noticed a chart listing the new fares, but for even numbers of tokens only.

"How about six?" the woman in the booth shouted into the microphone.

"Oh, no thanks," I replied. "I just need five today."

She scowled. "Well, how about four then? How about four or six?"

"I need five tokens, please."

"Well, you are a stubborn thing!" she shouted, shoving five tokens through the slot so fiercely that they fell to the floor.

So for any New Yorkers who have wondered what they'll get for the additional quarter, how about verbal abuse?

Rita D. Polidori

Sign Language

Sign, spotted by Judy Lerner of Jericho, Long Island, on the front door of a travel agency:

PLEASE GO AWAY.

.   .   .

Dear Diary:
  Sign, spotted in the produce department of a Food Lion supermarket, North Myrtle Beach, South Carolina:

IF YOU WISH SOMETHING YOU DON'T SEE,
ASK OUR PERISHABLE MANAGER.

I looked and looked for a Perishable Manager, but he or she had evidently expired.

Barbara D. Miltenberger

.　　.　　.

Listed under Religious Services in *The New York Times*, May 18, 1996, for Marble Collegiate Church:
" 'The Beauty and Power of Solitude'
"This Sunday at 11:15 A.M.—Everyone is welcome."

.　　.　　.

Sign, spotted by Milton Kaplan of Brooklyn Heights, in the window of a Bronx printing shop:

WEDDING INVITATIONS
PRINTED IN A HURRY

.　　.　　.

Hand-lettered cardboard sign seen by Jeffrey C. Loeser in the window of a deli on Eighteenth Avenue in Brooklyn:

FROZEN MILKY WAYS
FIRST OF THE SEASON

.   .   .

Announcement spotted by Roberta Klarreich of Brooklyn in Stagebill's calendar of events: "Oct. 3, New York City Opera: *The Return of the Screw* by Benjamin Britten."

The sequel, perhaps?

.   .   .

Sign, seen by Susan H. Llewellyn, displayed at the Museum of Television and Radio:

> VIRTUAL REALITY IS OUT
> OF SERVICE TODAY.
> SORRY FOR THE INCONVENIENCE.

.   .   .

Hand-lettered sign spotted by Arthur Witkin of Hartsdale, New York, taped to the information window of the office of the State Department of Motor Vehicles in White Plains:

> THE PERSON WHO SPEAKS ENGLISH
> WILL NOT BE IN TODAY.

.   .   .

Sign, spotted by Jim Fragale, in an apartment elevator on West Seventy-second Street:

FOUND IN ELEVATOR
ONE UGLY EARRING
CALL DON AT . . .

．　　　．　　　．

Dear Diary:

Leaving my Upper West Side apartment several days ago, I noticed that the warehouse-like store across the street, which had been vacant for some time, now had a tenant—temporarily, anyway—as well as a window sign, "Passover Products Available."

A truck was parked at the curb, and huge cardboard boxes containing Passover food were being carried into the store. A peek inside indicated extremely narrow aisles. One potential customer approached a truckman. "Where's your boss?" he asked.

The truckman thought for a while, mentally moving about the van. "OK," he said. "Go into the store down the first aisle, make a left at the egg matzohs, and a right at the gefilte fish."

Sandy Jaffe

．　　　．　　　．

Sign spotted in the exercise room of the West Side YMCA on Sixty-third Street:

AS A COURTESY TO OTHERS
PLEASE DO NOT SPIT
ON YOUR HANDS
BEFORE LIFTING WEIGHTS—SPORTS FITNESS

.   .   .

Sign, spotted by Emily A. Whitfield, in the window of a flower shop on Broadway and Twenty-third Street (and contender for the 1991 Who's on First Award).

BEGINNING SEPT. 17TH
BILL AND SUNNEE
FORMERLY OF DEAN AND JAY
WILL BE AT
JACK AND NICHOLAS HAIRSTYLING
ONE FLIGHT UP

.   .   .

Spotted by Catherine M. Conroy: a new Laundromat on Port Washington Boulevard in Port Wash-

ington, Long Island. A large window poster with black
letters announces:

> ALBERT IS HERE!
> FORMERLY OF THE
> LAUNDRY BASKET.

.   .   .

Sign spotted by Jerome B. Bonat on the door of the
Chinese Wok restaurant in Fort Lee, New Jersey:

> SORRY, WE DO NOT SERVE
> DIM SUM ON MOTHER'S DAY.

Grandes Dames

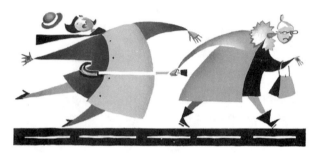

Dear Diary:

Bounding up Third Avenue doing my Saturday-morning errands, I passed a rather frail-looking elderly woman with a cane, standing on a corner. She called out to ask if I'd help her cross the street. I gave her my arm and proceeded at what I thought was an appropriate speed. Apparently it wasn't.

"Let's move it!" she said.

Catherine Barriger

. . .

Overheard while standing in line for *A Delicate Balance* at the Plymouth Theater on West Forty-fifth Street:

Young man in the box office: "I'm sorry, ma'am. We have no seats left for the Saturday-evening performance. But we do have some very good seats for the matinee."

Stately matron (after drawing herself up to her full height and before huffing away): "We are not a matinee family!"

Franklin J. Leicht

.　　.　　.

Dear Diary:

After he had helped a grateful elderly woman across a snowy Upper East Side street, I heard the young man say: "Actually, lady, I was kicked out of the Boy Scouts. Have a nice day!"

Chris Ford

.　　.　　.

Place: Grand Army Plaza, Central Park South and Fifth Avenue.

Dramatis personae: Well-dressed matron and equally well-dressed girl about five or six years old. Kenneth Kowald overhears their conversation as they stroll past the recently-spraying-but-now-dry fountain opposite the Plaza Hotel.

Little girl: "Grandmother, why isn't the fountain working today?"

Grandmother, glancing up at the statue: "We're all trying to conserve water, dear—even Mrs. Pulitzer."

.　　.　　.

The line was exceptionally long at a Chemical Bank branch in the upper reaches of the Bronx, even for a Friday afternoon when many working people come in to cash their paychecks. There was an increasing amount of impatience. A neatly dressed woman of a certain age arrived, went directly to the head of the line, and stood in front of the Select Banking window.

The brash young man who would have been next was apparently unaware that depositors with a certain substantial sum in their accounts can come to this window without having to wait on line. He protested loudly.

Unperturbed, the woman turned around and in the grandest of voices said, "The rewards of money!"

Milton H. Rosenberg

•　　•　　•

Letter from a movie-fan friend:

My contribution—if not solution—to the recent Diary entry on the subject of conduct unbecoming to art-house gentility:

I awoke early the other morning to catch the eleven-o'clock showing of *The Remains of the Day* at the Loews Paris theater in Manhattan.

The seats filled up quickly with others of my age group (the elderly four-dollar crowd). As the exquisite film unfolded, two women in back of me opened their aluminum-foil-covered lunch. Noisily.

Think fast. What's a seventy-six-year-old woman to do? How would Emily Post have handled this?

I turned around and murmured, "Stop rattling the paper or I will punch you out!"

I am delighted to report that quiet was instantly restored.

Clotheshorse

Dear Diary:

I was getting dressed to go to a couple of parties, enthusiastic about wearing a minidress I recently bought. I spent at least twenty minutes trying on a half-dozen belts, not certain which one, if any, looked best. I finally decided on the black one with the gold buckle. In the elevator a neighbor remarked, "Fabulous dress." The doorman told me I looked fantastic.

Then I hit the street. At the end of my driveway an elderly woman with a shopping cart laden with plastic bags sat resting on a box. She watched me walk down the driveway and I saw her twist all the way around so she could get a better look. Then she called out, "Take off the belt!"

I did. Messages from the universe are hard to ignore.

Karen Rosenberg

.   .   .

Dear Diary:

On one of those last sweltering summer days, fighting my usual instinct never to wear white in the city, I dressed in a white sweater and skirt for a "Mostly Mozart" concert at Lincoln Center. My outfit was color-coordinated by white-and-tan spectator pumps. At the last minute—not having the stamina to change purses—I slung my everyday black bag over my shoulder.

When I walked into the auditorium I was approached by an elegantly dressed woman.

"I noticed you on the crosstown bus," she said, "and I think your outfit is cool and lovely." I was extremely pleased with the compliment and getting ready to thank her when she looked me over once more and added, "But what's with the purse?"

Perhaps it's easier to wear black.

Sandy Harris

.   .   .

Dear Diary:

On an escalator at the High Street subway station in Brooklyn, I hear a young woman talking to a male acquaintance. She is dressed in regulation military camouflage fatigues, including a GI Joe cap, and is carrying a duffel bag.

"I chose not to wear my beret," she says. "You don't want to be too conspicuous in the subway."

Rudy D. Green

.　　.　　.

A short friend writes from Brooklyn Heights:

Some people watch birds. Some prefer the lower Manhattan skyline. But as a woman, I prefer the more entertaining spectacle of watching men crowd into the elevators in the mornings at the Clark Street subway station.

They are always impeccably dressed in Brooks Brothers, Paul Stuart, and sometimes Giorgio Armani. They're a serious and disciplined crew. You can tell that by 8:45 A.M. they've already read two newspapers, shampooed their hair, eaten a cholesterol-free breakfast, and spent at least forty-five minutes jogging.

But the close quarters of an elevator reveal all. And often what it reveals is a little aquamarine puff of shaving cream nestled softly beneath the earlobe. On further inspection, we notice that the faces of these carefully groomed titans of law and finance are decorated with tiny red speckles—usually beneath the sideburns or around the jawbone—which turn out to be shaving cuts.

These sightings may thwart style. But in a city where the very act of getting to work can seem treacherous, it is nice to know that there lurks a joyful and amusing pastime—one that in sheer subtlety and diversity surpasses even Audubon.

.   .   .

Dear Diary:

It was during an intermission before the final act of *La Traviata*, on the third-ring level. Two sturdy-looking women in their middle years were strolling and chatting. I overheard one of them say of Violetta, the heroine, in a tone of mild indignation tinged with resignation: "Sure, she's going to die in a beautiful peignoir. I don't even own a peignoir. I'm going to die in my sweat suit."

Later, I wondered whether there would have been an opera if Violetta had been a jogger.

Donald J. Kahn

.   .   .

Scene: Filene's basement.

Dramatis personae: Man and woman inspecting a scarf.

He: "But does it have enough oomph for her?"

Oomph! That very word made me smile and bathed me in nostalgia. I had the urge to rush home and play an Ann Sheridan film. Instead I bought the scarf for myself. One can never have too much oomph, especially at Christmas.

G. Lehrer

.   .   .

Dear Diary:

This morning at the C train Forty-second Street stop I saw a blind man who seemed confused about where to go. I approached him and asked if he needed help. He said he wanted to go to the Port Authority Bus Terminal.

When he took my arm so that I could help him, he felt my coat sleeve and asked what kind of coat I was wearing.

"Fur," I said.

"Shame on you," he replied.

Beverly Dolinsky

.   .   .

Dear Diary:

When my ninety-four-year-old neighbor complained that her slip and fall on her carpeted floor was caused by her "slippery slippers," I suggested she wear shoes even in her apartment. Somewhat indignantly, she shot back: "Shoes? Shoes? With my robe? I'd rather die! Don't forget, I was a dress designer!"

Elizabeth Williger

. . .

The morning following our fairy-tale wedding at the Essex House, my new husband woke and stared out at the magnificent view of Central Park from our bridal suite on the thirty-fourth floor. Then he became very quiet and said, "Honey, I don't know if I should tell you this or not..."

I joined him at the window to see what had horrified him so.

"It looks like one of the carriage horses died," he said.

Sure enough, by the curb of Central Park South, police cars surrounded a horse lying stiffly on the ground.

We watched the scene for several minutes more—passersby stopping, tourists staring, the hansom-cab driver in top hat kneeling beside her animal—and tried to figure out what this omen could possibly mean for our marriage, as well as for animal-rights activists.

Suddenly the driver snapped her fingers. With that, the horse stood up and began happily munching from a bucket of oats. On closer inspection, we made out the figures of a photographer, stylist, and makeup person.

Just another talented horse earning his feed in the glamorous world of modeling.

Marisa Cohen

Seasonings

. . .

HERE COMES MARCH

What, again? that sulky month
neither winter nor spring
like a bad-tempered adolescent girl
who, not knowing her own mind
cries one day, is hysterical the next,
takes up her Cinderella broom of rain,
spitefully sweeps hats off our heads,
turns umbellas inside out,
floods avenues and highways
until the wind, losing patience with her antics,
pushes her right out of the calendar.

Hannah Alexander

Dear Diary:

An awful New York night with every street corner an obstacle course of snow and slush. Regardless, we were determined to go to the symphony at Avery Fisher Hall. In a last-minute effort to organize coats, scarfs, briefcases, etc., I clenched the tickets in my teeth.

As I approached the usher, he said pointedly, "Sir, we do not take tickets from people's mouths."

Bob Overlock

. . .

APRIL

After so long
hardly anyone remembers:
April's air
is colder than November's
But April is like
a pitcher warming up:

gradually the ball
starts to hop.

Ed Rosemann

. . .

Scene: West Ninety-sixth Street, the day after the blizzard. A woman and her son—about seven or eight—are scrutinizing the mounds of snow as they walk up the street. The boy is dragging his feet and complaining.

"It's here somewhere," the woman said. "You know we can't go home until we find it."

Assuming they had dropped something in the snow, Joelle G. White asked what she had lost.

"My car," she said.

.   .   .

A friend writes:

A few weeks ago I went back to the Long Island beach town where I spent summers of my childhood. It was the Fourth of July weekend and I was feeling a bit melancholy. I hoped the sights and sounds and smells of the seashore, the boardwalk, and streets I had known so well would bring back a rush of happy memories.

I walked by my old grammar school (now a condominium). I wandered past the movie theater where I had worked as an usher in deliciously "air-cooled" darkness during my high school years, when movies seemed glorious and the moviegoers thanked me when I flashed my light and showed them to their seats. The theater—it was called simply, lovingly, the Laurel—is, of course, now closed, its marquee sagging sadly, the front boarded up, probably forever.

On the boardwalk, fortresslike condos and co-ops rise where tacky, glitzy, blue-mirrored arcades with names like Funland, Skiball, and Fascination echoed with screams of delight and the joyous sound of buzzers indicating that a prize was now yours. And there were the rides that zoomed you to the starry skies above and back again.

That weekend, though, even the delighted giggles of children at the shore seemed more muted than I had remembered. The ocean was clear but cold. I sat in the sun with a friend and thought about todays and tomorrows and, above all, yesterdays. I think I hardly spoke at all.

When the sun softened and it came time to leave, we gathered our belongings. On the short walk from the beach to the Long Island Rail Road train that would take us back to Manhattan, we passed two boys, maybe seven or eight years old, who had set up an impromptu stand near a home on whose lawn hydrangeas were beginning to bloom.

"Excuse me, sirs," one of the youngsters said softly. "Would you care to buy some lemonade? It's very cold." His voice was almost pleading. With only minutes to spare to catch our train, we continued on. "Not today," I said, a bit too brusquely, perhaps, without breaking stride.

It wasn't till we were on the way back to New York, watching towns whizzing by, that I thought about the youngsters and their lemonade and how I wished we had stopped and purchased a cup and told them how refreshing it was. Behind sunglasses I began to weep silently—for the passing summers, for all the kids grown-ups too often ignore, for all their hopes and dreams and the lemonade they never sell.

I've returned to the beach every weekend since then, but I have not seen the boys and their pitchers of lemonade again.

.   .   .

JULY FOURTH NIGHTS

Back when summer used to start
as suddenly as a firecrackered sky
we would explode tin cans with
cherry bombs and chase freckle-faced girls
with hissing sparklers and
all the while, dream the dreams of
children who pretend to own their futures.
Of driving fast cars down slow streets
or laughing in love beneath the stars and
stripes of endless July Fourth nights.
And looking somewhere beyond the
bright booms and loud lights we clutched
at red, white, and blue fantasies of
growing up, but never growing old.

Roger Granet

.   .   .

Dear Diary:

It's a hot and sticky night at the tail end of a summer that has gone on too long. The suburban New Jersey neighborhood is pitch black and everyone's windows are open to catch any hint of a breeze.

Perhaps in an effort to make the summer last, my eleven-year-old son steps onto the screened porch, his saxophone in tow, and bids goodnight to the neighborhood with a slow, mournful rendition of "Taps." The notes linger in the darkness.

Out of the night comes the sound of a single pair of hands applauding his performance. Then, from somewhere in the distance, through the blackness, we hear a faint echo: the sound of someone else's "Taps" drifting toward us from an anonymous trumpet in the late-summer night.

Peggy Heller

.   .   .

Dear Diary:

The temperature in Central Park had soared to 102 degrees. Gus the polar bear was sweating it even more than usual. And then I heard the sounds of the Delacorte Clock playing . . . "Jingle Bells." The work of a subversive clock master? The heat didn't seem so unbearable after all.

Jonathan Kuhn

.   .   .

AUTUMN ALIVE

Summer's a noun that lies dozing
In butter-warm hours,
In bee-song and flowers
In leaf-cool—shhh, do not disturb
Till Autumn. But Autumn's a verb!
It wakes and it hustles,
It rustles, it bustles,
It's scarlet at tree-top and curb,
It's spiced like an apple, an herb. . . .
If August's a noun,
Half-asleep, lying down,
October's most surely a verb!

Maureen Cannon

.　　.　　.

Dear Diary:

Place: A snow-filled, almost-deserted upper Broadway.

Time: The morning after the big blizzard.

A mother is holding a Food Emporium shopping bag in one hand and her young son's hand in her other. The boy, about six, is commenting newscast-style about what is going on.

"It's a blizzard," he says. "See that car? It's stuck. Really stuck. The roads are very bad. It's an emergency."

A pause before the worst news of all: "The people who want to go to East Hampton can't get there."

Marian Decker

.   .   .

CHANGES

Every now and so often
the wind shifts
and the sun, although warm,
lengthens her shadows.
A calm drifts along city streets
stealing from trees their
green aroma.
A waiting time . . .
September inhales her breath,
purses her lips
and blows out another
   summer.

Doris Klein

.   .   .

Dear Diary:

It's been a tough, wet, cool spring throughout the East, especially hard on baseball. Games have been postponed on account of rain, wet grounds, even snow.

But as usual, in New York it was something entirely unexpected.

The West Side Little League Pee Wee Division plays its games on concrete diamonds in Riverside Park near the Boat Basin. The field is lined with beautiful flowering cherry trees, now past their prime. A few Saturdays ago, a furious gust of wind from off the Hudson stirred up a dense cloud of cherry blossoms that left a half-inch of blossoms on the field.

"Time out," yelled the volunteer umpire. And players, coaches, and parents had no choice but to enjoy our first encounter with a pink-out.

After one more cherry blossom pink-out, the wind died down and the boys and girls were able to finish the game.

Roger M. Kubarych

Seeing Stars

Dear Diary:

The other afternoon I saw Mary on Central Park West! I was walking with my young daughter and wished I had worn something less frumpy. Mary—there's only one, of course—was alone and she looked great with a new shorter hairdo. I couldn't believe it had been twenty years since she first met Rhoda, Phyllis, Ted, Murray, and the rest of the gang that kept me happily at home on those pre-VCR Saturday nights. They were some of the nicest nights of my single days!

I confided as much to my daughter, who had the good sense not to ask, "Mary who?" She did, however, emit an embarrassed "Oh, Mother!" after I had managed a shy "Hello, Mary" to my idol as she sprinted by.

Mary flashed a warm, wide-eyed smile which I'm sure meant "Hi there."

"You're wonderful," I said. Or something like that.

"Oh, Mother!" my daughter said again.

"Wait, just wait!" I told her. And I smiled again. This time not at Mary, but at the thought of my daughter, walking somewhere in Manhattan with her daughter years from now and spotting a silver-haired woman strolling along in something snug-fitting and lacy.

"Oh wow! Cool!" my daugher will say. Or something like that.

Her daughter will look extremely puzzled.

"Madonna!" my daughter will explain excitedly. "It's Madonna! She used to sing and dance. She was my very favorite. I've got to say hello."

"Oh, Mother!" her daughter will say.

Or at least I hope she will.

Carolyn Hanson

. . .

Today I met Mary! I was strolling to work enjoying spring when I spotted a lovely blonde. "It's Mary!" I thought.

She was about to enter a restaurant with a man— I'm not sure if it was Peter or Paul—and I just had to go up to speak to the woman who had made my teenage years so happy.

"You are Mary, aren't you?" I asked, just to be sure. No last name was necessary, of course.

She smiled. "Yes, I am," she said. I told her I'd loved her for thirty years. She said she hoped I'd have a good day.

Dorothy Rosenberg

.　　.　　.

It was one of the final warm golden days of the season and our friend-about-town was lunching outside Good and Plenty on West Forty-third Street near Ninth Avenue. Peering up from her pasta salad, she saw—be still, my heart—Al Pacino walking toward her. The actor, looking very Armani, was accompanied by a friendly golden-haired dog whose leash was a nifty necktie.

The two joined a group of movie types at a nearby table. A few minutes later, Mr. Pacino excused himself and headed inside the restaurant. After a few steps, he turned around and said, politely but firmly: "Sit! Wait! I'll be back." Dog or no dog, our friend insists that Mr. Pacino was looking directly at her when he gave his command.

At any rate, the last time we saw her she was still sitting and waiting.

.　　.　　.

Charlotte Chandler was walking along Fifth Avenue when she heard her name being called. Turning around, she saw a man holding a copy of *Hello I Must Be Going*, the book about Groucho Marx she wrote a few years ago.

"I just had to tell you how much I like your book," the man said. "I just loved Groucho, and I hope you don't mind my stopping you like this."

Miss Chandler said she didn't mind at all.

"I don't want to keep you," the man continued, "but I wonder if you would autograph my book."

A glowing Miss Chandler reached for the book and began to compose a few words in her mind. She was stopped in midthought. The book was stamped "New York Public Library."

. . .

Dear Diary:

Honeymooning in Manhattan on a brilliant Sunday afternoon in early autumn. We left the Whitney and turned down Madison Avenue. Then, wow! Half a block away I spotted Barbra Bigger-Than-Life Streisand heading toward me, swinging two golden shopping bags, her stylish coat open to the fresh breeze!

What to say to her? Request an autograph? Ask an engaging question?

But wait a minute! There are dozens of Sunday strollers on this block. Don't they recognize Barbra Streisand?

Suddenly, a feeling from out of the past swept over me, a feeling I had known decades back when I, too, was a New Yorker. And I knew what to do. I hugged my bride close to me.

And as Barbra brushed by me, I looked coolly down Madison Avenue and simply ignored her.

Edward W. Campion, M.D.

.   .   .

Dear Diary:

The other clear and beautiful morning, I was walking west on East Seventy-ninth Street. Approaching from the other direction were a mother and father and a boy about seven, obviously their son.

I happened to focus on the youngster as we neared each other, and I chuckled because he was a dead ringer for Art Garfunkel—from the frizzy blondish hair that sprang out defiantly in every direction to the whimsical half-smile on his intelligent face. A striking resemblance, I said to myself.

That's when I looked up and saw that the boy's father was Art Garfunkel. It was as if the boy were announcing, wordlessly and by his very countenance: Next generation of Garfunkels in place, all present and accounted for. Somehow, all seemed right with the world.

Jeffrey Newman

Underground Exchanges

The last car of an IRT No. 1 local traveling south from Ninety-sixth Street. Two muscular construction workers in their mid-thirties and sporting baseball caps, brims turned to the back, are chewing the fat.

Construction worker One, unwrapping a stick of Black Jack: "You know, this is a very famous gum."

Construction worker Two: "Oh, yeah?"

One: "Yeah, they made it all the way back in the 1930s."

Two: "So?"

One, shoving gum in his mouth: "Ginger Rogers and Fred Astaire chewed it when they danced."

Two: "They could chew and dance, too?"

Richard De Thuin

. . .

Gene Tashoff of Larchmont, New York, is concealing his smile behind a newspaper while straphanging in Manhattan. The cause of his amusement: two weary "working girl" types, former coworkers reunited by a chance encounter on the platform. They are sharing updates.

Woman One: "So what are you making?"
Woman Two: "Me? Eighteen thousand. And you?"
Woman One: "Lasagna."

.   .   .

Dear Diary:

It is 5:00 P.M. Friday on a No. 2 train riding uptown from Wall Street. I am sandwiched between two young women conversing about a recent trip to Europe.

"Then we were off to Italy," one says to the other. "Pisa, Assisi, Rome, and Florence. Rome was my favorite."

My attention is hooked: Rome has become one of my favorite places because of its rich history and ruins.

She continues:

"You know, it's so modern. I mean, there's the Colosseum and the Forum, but the tiles on our hotel bathroom floor were to die for! And those room keys—you know, the ones that open the doors with a plastic card?" Her friend nods with enthusiasm.

I smile, realizing our perspectives of Rome are different

indeed. As I leave the train at 14th Street, I hear the conversation continue: "Now Florence, Florence is old."

Aileen Panke

.   .   .

Dear Diary:

I was in the shuttle, waiting what always seems an eternity for it to take me from Grand Central to Times Square. A woman next to me called through the still-open door to a man on the platform.

Woman: "Victor! Victor! You look confused. Where do you want to go?"

Man: "I want to go to Paris, but this train doesn't go there."

The doors closed, and as we lurched toward the West Side, for a moment my life was filled with endless possibilities.

Marc Fine

.   .   .

Dear Diary:

I was on a southbound No. 4 train; bits of conversations wafted by. Somewhere between Fourteenth Street and the Brooklyn Bridge, I heard two young women—they obviously knew each other but had not seen one another for some time—catching up on things.

Woman One: "Do you remember Kathy Coffee?"

Woman Two: "Sure I do!"

Woman One: "Well, she married a guy named Steve Potts and now her name is Kathy Coffee Potts!"

Everyone smiled and that made my commute just a little nicer.

Dolores Rode

.　　　.　　　.

The scene: a Lexington Avenue subway platform.

Dramatis personae: Jayne Brookes and the two women whose conversation she hears. The topic is names.

Woman One: "What about Michael? Michael's a nice name."

Woman Two: "Oh, yes! Michael is good. It goes with everything."

.　　　.　　　.

Overheard on a Brooklyn-bound local, one woman straphanger to another: "She thought he asked her out for a Hawaiian dinner. It turned out to be a Houlihan's."

Parades

To be filed under O as in Only in the Village on Halloween. Barred from visiting Harry Houdini's grave earlier in the day because, they were told, only members of the Magicians' Union were allowed near his tomb (Houdini died on Halloween), David Cross and Robert Bent headed for the Three Lives and Company bookstore in Greenwich Village for the signing of their new book, *Dead Ends: An Irreverent Field Guide to the Graves of the Famous*. Just as the signing was concluding, a Joan Crawford impersonator rushed into the store.

"I'm lost! I'm lost! Where's my grave?"

"Ferncliff Mausoleum in Westchester," Mr. Bent said matter-of-factly. The Crawford lookalike said thank you and then ran back into the night to parade with other ghouls and goblins.

. . .

Dear Diary:

Watching the Halloween parade at Twenty-first Street and Avenue of the Americas, I overheard a woman dressed as a chicken ask the fellow beside her, "Did you see a pink genie and a man dressed like a priest?" He said that he had not.

The chicken persisted. "They were behind the killer bees." The man shook his head. She sighed. "Oh, well, they can find their own way home."

Janice Whelan

. . .

Letter from our friend the couch potato:

Maybe sometimes service gets better after all. Take cable TV. When I used to call Manhattan Cable to question the quality of reception, in my best Prince Charming voice, it seemed as if I always got Grumpy, Sleepy, or Dopey on the other end. But the company is now called Time Warner Cable, and things are looking up a bit. The service representatives, for instance. Boy, are they chatty! At least the woman I spoke to the other afternoon was.

"Pardon me, but just where is Charles Street?" she wanted to know when I gave her my address. Greenwich Village, I told her. "Oh, that's an awful place to drive," she said. "We got caught in the Halloween parade and missed half of Henny Youngman."

"Henny Youngman was in the Halloween parade?"

"No," she said. "He was in Brooklyn and we were driving to hear him. Do you like Henny?"

"I'm getting tired of stand-up comedians," I confessed.

"Channel 4 is really bad in the part of Brooklyn where I live," she said.

"Complain to your bosses," I suggested.

"I don't have cable," she said. That seemed to terminate our conversation. "It sure was nice talking to you," she said. "See you in a parade."

"Give my best to Henny," I said.

Click. Gone forever. But perhaps other new friends await me at Time Warner? True, there's always Geraldo, Joan, Jane, Jenny, Phil, Oprah, Sally Jessy, Maury, and Montel.

Still, there was something special about my brief interlude with the Henny Youngman fan out there in Cable Land.

.   .   .

I learned last week that in New York there's no better place to make friends than at a parade. Watching the welcome home for our troops from my choice spot in front of Trinity Church—I arrived from South Orange at 9:30 A.M. and stayed until the very end—I met Mary and Marilyn from Jersey City and we immediately began calling ourselves the three M's (my name is Marion).

The first hero we saw was piled with ham, salami, cheese, lettuce, and tomato and wrapped in cellophane. It was someone's lunch. Then there was the little girl who threatened to upchuck if her mother and grandmother didn't get her to the front row. A middle-aged couple from Allentown, Pennsylvania, brought little stools to sit on and offered them to Mary and Marilyn when the New Jersey ladies felt faint. People gladly shared their bottled water.

The woman from Allentown told Marilyn to stand on the stool just as General Schwarzkopf passed by. One of the legs broke and Marilyn fell. She was OK, though, and so we all laughed. We counted balloons and the colors of confetti.

At 3:30 P.M., Marilyn and Mary kissed me on the cheek and said, "We old gals are leaving now. We had a great time." By 5:15, the woman in front of me with the yellow ribbons around her wrist and three American flags planted in her hair was the only one left from our original group. As I started to leave she shouted out to me, "See you at the next parade!"

Marion Balavenber

Celebrations, Etc.

I am not home today. The door is locked, the shades are drawn, the answering machine is on. It is a gray, drizzly, damp day. I have decided not to meet the world.

It is the kind of day that most people greet with groans when the alarm goes off and they are forced to get up, get dressed, and go out the front door while the dog or cat is still curled in a ball content to continue dreaming.

Today I have decided to say no to traffic jams, lengthy lists of things to do, time pressures, demands. No hurried breakfast or lunch today. I am content to be alone. The door is closed to neighbors, repairmen, meter inspectors. Nor can I be reached by phone: my machine politely tells each caller that I cannot come to the phone right now but promise to get back later.

But not today, I smile, for today is my day to turn my back to the wake-up music that spiritedly comes from my clock radio. I turn a deaf ear to my husband's nervous "When are you getting up?" I drift, instead, in and out of a smooth, blue, billowy sea. I bask beneath an island sun.

Today, then, is my day to dream, to declare a holiday on this ordinary, middle-of-the-week day, and to wonder what all the rush is about outside.

Maryanne M. Garbowsky

. . .

Dear Diary:

We cannot wait to hear about Gary's kindergarten play this year. Two years ago, his school put on *Snow White*, with twenty-seven "dwarfs," so more of the children could be in the play. Last year, it presented *The Nativity*. Joseph came to the inn and knocked on the door. The little boy playing the innkeeper decided to be inventive. When Joseph asked if there was room at the inn, he answered by saying:

"You are so lucky. We have just had a cancellation."

Maxine Marron

The place: Bloomingdale's.
The time: Some afternoons ago. Ted Bacon, brows-

ing through greeting cards, finds several that extend Happy Earth Day wishes.

"Just when is Earth Day?" Mr. Bacon asks the clerk.

"I don't know," the sweet young thing replies with a shrug of her shoulders. "I work in notions."

.   .   .

GOODBYE, OLD YEAR

I crept past Father Time
while he was distracted
by funny hats, noisemakers,
balloons and bells.
As soon as he was out of my sight
I hurried faster
than I thought I could.
I had escaped his scythe.
Hurrah! It is now 12:01!

Beatrice Comas

.   .   .

FATHER'S DAY

Sipping coffee
from the partly painted
almost glazed coffee mug

that you made
for Father's Day
too many years ago

I think of
soccer games, school plays
and scraped knees

and when everyone
leaves the breakfast table
I turn the cup upside down

and staring at your
third-grade fingerprints and
crooked ceramic signature

I smile
while finishing my morning
mug of memories.

Roger Granet

Modem Times

Dear Diary:

Walking down the street in Maplewood, New Jersey, on an early-spring day, I happen upon a father and his five-year-old son. Running ahead, the youngster screeches to a halt at the corner and calls to his father, "Which way?"

"To the right," the father responds.

The youngster looks down at his hands, trying to remember which one is his right hand, and I hear Dad call out, "You know, the one you move the mouse with!"

The boy immediately waves his right hand and skips up the street on his right.

Peggy Barnett

.   .   .

Virginia Miles of Englewood, New Jersey, has just given her order to a woman behind the counter at her neighborhood McDonald's. The counterwoman is having difficulty totaling the order on her register.

"Darn it," she says, "this machine is broken. I'll have to figure this out the old-fashioned way." With that, she reaches into a drawer and pulls out a calculator.

.　　.　　.

Dear Diary:

A pregnant friend filling out preadmissions forms for Beth Israel Medical Center identifies as her next of kin her companion, who is also the father of her child. Asked for his relationship to her, she writes, "True love."

Days later, the office calls, saying, "Our computer does not recognize true love."

Lisa K. Eastwood

.　　.　　.

The scene: The Midtown office of a large Manhattan corporation.

The cast: Two muscular men—one a new employee, another a two-year veteran.

New: "Do you work out?"

Vet: "Every chance I get. Weekends at the gym, home whenever possible. I have a set of dumbbells, ranging from ten to fifty pounds each."

New: "Me, too."
Thirty seconds later:
New: "Do you take your laptop computer home every night?"
Vet: "No, it's too heavy. Must weigh almost six pounds."
New: "Me, too."

Bradley Bealle

You once knew writers were at work
By the sound of their typewriters.
Daytimes in the spring or summer,
Whole streets in the Village
And on the West Side were filled
With the music of clacking and bells.
Now there is silence—windows closed
For air-conditioning, computers
Beeping too quietly to be heard
Below. It may be possible to compose
Even poems on computer screens,
But something in me doubts it.
Yet even quills dipped in ink
And scratching across parchment
Were a technological advance
Over chanting voices in firelight
And with the same purpose: Understanding
Our fears as the shadows grow.

Lewis Gardner

. . .

Dear Diary:

As the mother of a three-year-old, certain things come as no surprise. But yesterday's phone call really threw me. My son, David, called his friend Jillian, and this is what followed:

"Hi, this is David. Is Jillian there? . . . Well, is her mommy home? . . . Is Jeff there?" (Jeff is Jillian's father.) "Do you know when she'll be home?"

All of his questions were being fielded by the baby-sitter caring for Jillian's sister, Cloe. When it became clear that David was not going to connect with Jillian he asked, "Well, then, can I have Jillian's voice mail?"

Diane Oshin

. . .

Dear Diary:

My thirty-something son was showing a newly acquired computer to his six-year-old son. Together, they composed a story and entered it. The father pressed a key and the screen went blank. He pressed another key and the story reappeared on the screen. The six-year-old gleefully embraced the machine.

"I love you, computer," he said. "You remembered my story."

Joel H. Joseph

City Souvenirs

BROOKLYN BASEBALL

As a kid, me and my best friend
Jerry caught a night game at
Ebbets Field and watched the Dodgers
beat the Giants just before da Bums
abandoned us and beat it out of Town.

Podres was unstoppable, a smooth
southpaw with a slippery slider.

And Junior Gilliam ate up every
grounder at second with the graceful
gait of a gifted ballet dancer.

Peanuts and pop-ups held our hearts.
And in the ninth, Campanella hit
a homer so high that I knew New York
owned every star in the sky and that
baseball belonged to Brooklyn forever.

Roger Granet

.   .   .

CARNEGIE HALL, 1960

At seventeen I came to New York. The dormitory
Was higher than most buildings I'd ever
Been in. I ate in a coffee shop
Where people never looked at you,
Went on a tour of Bellevue
Because it was a place, like Lindy's
Or the Metropolitan Museum of Art,
So legendary that being there was magic.
Some New York kids I met said,
"Let's go to Carnegie Hall." From Standing Room
We looked down at the Philharmonic
And their TV-star conductor, jumping
Up and down on his podium, all creating
Wonderful noise that filled the place
And vibrated to the roots of my hair.
The things you could take for granted in New York!

Lewis Gardner

.   .   .

A friend writes:

Growing up on Long Island, I longed for an apartment of my own in Greenwich Village. Not the Village as it was then (this was the 1950s) but as it had been in the thirties and forties, an era of coffeehouses, checkered tablecloths, candles dripping in Chianti bottles, glamour. Symbolizing the Village for me most of all was the Village Vanguard on Seventh Avenue South, home of jazz musicians and smart sophisticated on-their-way-to-fame entertainers like Betty Comden, Adolph Green, and Judy Holliday, who were part of a group called the Revuers, performing smart 1940s sophisticated songs and patter. Oh, to perform there. Oh, to write smart 1940s sophisticated songs and patter.

Flash-forward twenty years or so: I move to the Village, and wonder of wonders, my apartment is across the avenue from the Vanguard. Bracketed now between a pizza parlor and a Chicken Lickin, the canopied building is still an exciting symbol of bohemia.

Which brings us to a week or so ago. On my way to the bank, my paycheck slipped out of my jacket pocket. Payment was stopped; still, it was an unsettling experience. Late that afternoon my phone rang. "Hello," a friendly voice said. "This is Mrs. Gordon of the Village Vanguard." Fame at last, I thought. "We found your paycheck," she said. Well, that was good news, too. The check, with my address on it, had blown across the avenue and landed in front of the Vanguard. "We like to watch out for our neighbors," Mrs. Gordon said, "and we're glad you're one of them."

.   .   .

REMEMBERING JAMAICA BAY

The gulls knife the air with a cry like a child's in
    the
night, gather in a white startle of wing-beats,
    then
whisper-brush the water. Something in that
    moment stabs me
and takes me to Jamaica Bay.

Nearly nine, I squint against a claret sun and
    watch my
mother swim out until her bathing cap is a white
    spot
bobbing like cork over each swell bruised purple
    under a
burnt sky. I think she is swimming to where sky
    and water
touch, to where she can't hear me. Inside my
    heart I am
pleading, turn back, come back, come back, and
    mouthing in a
hoarse whisper, please.

I wait until finally my mother floats in the
    shallows

breathless and happy, her white cap shiny with salt and
water and her skin scented with bay.

Patricia Viale Wuest

. . .

THE PHONE BOOTH

There are a few places,
Mostly old-fashioned candy stores,
Where you can call home
Behind closed doors;
And talk like you used to
Before those large glass walls
and that round padded seat
Went the way of the five-cent
Conversation.

Ellen Fuchs

. . .

"What about my pie?" the old woman called, knocking on the little glass door. "What about my pie?"

There was no answer. The door stayed shut, and the old woman never did get her pie.

I remember this every time I get nostalgic about the Automat.

Ed Rossmann

Last Words

Dear Diary:

Being a native New Yorker and proud of it, I found that having to move to Los Angeles was accompanied by extremes of upset and depression, relieved only by the prospect of getting to spend time with other former New Yorkers of my acquaintance who had already moved there.

One of them, my friend Mel, called soon after my arrival, with the intention of taking me on a lovely drive to Palm Springs. He inquired whether I had ever seen the desert in bloom.

I immediately responded that I had not seen it, did not know who was in it, and had not even read the reviews, but that if he thought it was worth seeing, to go ahead and get tickets.

After a long pause, Mel emitted a long, low whistle

and said slowly, "Some adjustments do take a bit longer than others."

Judith Katten

. . .

Dear Diary:

Next week I will graduate and leave New York. In the four years that I have lived here I never quite felt like a real New Yorker because I never saw Woody! Back in Oklahoma, filling out my applications to NYU, I would dream about my chance encounter with this legend, an experience I took to be requisite; what New Yorker, after all, hasn't at one time or another bumped into his bespectacled fellow? Time was running out for this coed.

Then last week, I dropped my graduation invitations into the mailbox. As I turned, whom did I find myself face to face with but the diminutive director himself? Our eyes met and we smiled. For the briefest moment, we stood, not as fan and hero, but as neighbors, two New Yorkers enjoying the warmth of spring.

I went on my way, confident that now I could leave New York feeling as if I had actually lived there. Farewell.

Margaret Gilbert